Nick Vandome

Laptops
for Seniors

in
easy steps

For the Over 50s

In easy steps is an imprint of In Easy Steps Limited
Southfield Road · Southam
Warwickshire CV47 0FB · United Kingdom
www.ineasysteps.com

Notice of Liability
Every effort has been made to ensure that this book
contains accurate and current information. However,
In Easy Steps Limited and the author shall not be liable
for any loss or damage suffered by readers as a result of
any information contained herein.

Trademarks
All trademarks are acknowledged as belonging to their
respective companies.

Printed and bound in the United Kingdom

ISBN-13 978-1-84078-342-1
ISBN-10 1-84078-342-7

Contents

1 Choosing a laptop

More and more computer users are now turning to laptops because of their convenience and portability. This chapter looks at some of the issues to consider when buying a laptop and how to ensure you buy the right one for your needs. It also covers the elements of a laptop and some of the accessories you will need.

A brief history of laptops

Modern computers have come a long way since the days of mainframe computers that took up entire rooms and were generally only the domain of large educational establishments or government organizations. Before microprocessors (the chips that are used to run modern-day computers) these mainframe computers were usually operated by punch-cards: the operators programmed instructions via holes in a punch-card and then waited for the results, which could take hours or days.

The first personal computers, i.e. ones in which all of the computing power was housed in a single box, started to appear in the early 1970s and the first machine that bore any resemblance to modern personal computers was called the Datapoint 2200. The real breakthrough for personal computers came with the introduction of microprocessors – small chips that contained all of the necessary processing power for the computer. After this the industry expanded at a phenomenal rate with the emergence of major worldwide companies such as Microsoft, Apple, IBM, Dell and Intel.

But even as soon as personal computers were being developed for a mass-market audience, there was a concerted drive to try and create a portable computer so that people could take their own computer with them wherever they went. Even in the fast moving world of technology the timescale for shrinking a computer from the size of a large room to the size of a small briefcase was a dramatic one.

First portable computers

With most types of technology we are obsessed with the idea of making the item as small as possible, whether it is a music player, a telephone or a computer. However, the first portable computers bore little resemblance to the machines that we now know as laptops. At the beginning of the 1980s there were a few portable computers released, but most of these were bulky, had very small screens and could not run on internal batteries. The most popular of these was called the Osborne 1, which was released in 1981. Although this

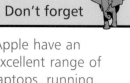

Don't forget

Apple have an excellent range of laptops, running their OS X operating system. However, the majority of this book deals with "IBM-compatible" laptops, as they are known. These types of laptops are the most common and run on the Windows operating system.

was the size of a small suitcase and had a minuscule amount of computing power compared with modern machines, it proved a big success as it enabled people to carry their computer around with them for the first time.

The machine that first used the term "laptop" was called the Gallian SC, which was developed in 1983 and introduced in 1984. This had the big advantage of being able to run on an internal battery and it was also one of the first portable computers that appeared with the now-universal "clamshell" design, where the monitor folded down over the keyboard.

In the late 1980s companies such as Kyocera, Tandy, Olivetti, NEC, IBM, Toshiba, Compaq and Zenith Data Systems began developing fast and more powerful laptops and it is in this period that the growth of laptops really began to take off.

In 1991 Apple introduced its PowerBook range of laptops, versions of which continue to be very successful, and in 1995 the introduction of Windows 95 provided an operating system that could be used in all IBM-compatible laptops.

Laptops have now become an integral part of the computer market and in some areas sales have outstripped those of desktop computers. Although the power and speed of laptops is not quite the same as that of the most powerful desktops, they are still more than capable of comfortably meeting the computing needs of most computer users. Add to this their portability (which has reached a stage in terms of size and weight such that you no longer need to worry about doing yourself an injury in order to carry one around) and it is clear why laptops have become so popular.

There are now a wide range of laptops on the market, which go by a variety of terms such as notebooks or ultraportables, and their power and versatility ensure that they are an excellent option for anyone who wants to have significant computing power at their fingertips wherever they are.

Don't forget

Because of their size and weight, the first portable computers, such as the Osborne 1, were known rather unflatteringly as "luggables".

Laptops v. desktops

When considering buying a laptop computer one of the first considerations is how it will perform in comparison with a desktop computer. In general, you will pay more for a laptop with similar specifications to a desktop. The reason for this is purely down to size: it is more expensive to fit the required hardware into a laptop than the more generous physical capacity of a desktop computer. However, with modern computing technology and power, even laptops with lower specifications than their desktop cousins will be able to handle all but the most intensive computing needs of most home users. The one situation where laptops will have to have as high a specification as possible is if you are going to be doing a lot a video downloading and editing, such as converting and editing old family movies.

Some of the issues to consider when looking at the differences between laptops and desktops are:

- Portability. Obviously, laptops easily win over desktops in this respect but when looking at this area it is worth thinking about how portable you actually want your computer to be. If you want to mainly use it in the home then you may think that a desktop is the answer. However, a laptop gives you portability in the home too, which means that you can use your computer in a variety of locations within the home and even in the garden, if desired

- Power. Even the most inexpensive laptops have enough computing power to perform most of the tasks that the majority of users require. However, if you want to have the same computing power as the most powerful desktops, then you will have to pay a comparatively higher price

- Functionality. Again, because of their size, desktops have more room for items such as DVD writers, multi-card readers and web-cams. These can be included with laptops but this can also increase the price and the weight of the laptop

Don't forget

Another issue with laptops is battery power, which is required to keep them operating when they are removed from a mains electrical source. Obviously, this is not an issue that affects desktops.

Types of laptops

To meet the needs of the different groups who use laptops there are several variations that are available:

- Ultraportables. These are very small laptops and are generally favored by business users. They have screens that are less than 12 inches (measured diagonally from corner to corner) and they usually weigh less than 1.7 kg. In addition, their keyboards are usually smaller than full-size ones. Sub-notebooks are similar to ultraportables, but usually slightly larger

- Small laptops. These are the smallest type of fully-featured laptops. They have screens of 12–14 inches (measured diagonally from corner to corner) and weigh 2–3 kg. They are a good option if you are going to be using your laptop a lot for traveling. Although a 12-inch screen may sound very small they are actually surprisingly effective

- Mid-range laptops. These are the most common types of laptops as they have a good combination of size, weight and power. They generally have screens that are approximately 15 inches (measured diagonally from corner to corner) and weigh 2.8–3.5 kg. These are an excellent option for using in the home and also while traveling

- Desktop replacements. These are large, heavier laptops that can be used in the home instead of a desktop computer. They are faster and more powerful than other types of laptops but the downside is that they are not as portable. They generally have screens that are 17 inches (measured diagonally from corner to corner) and weigh approximately 4–8 kg. Although these types of machines are very powerful, one of their main functions is for playing the latest computer games or watching movies. For the needs of the majority of laptop users the mid-range machines will be more than powerful enough and they are also a lot more portable

Hot tip

Try and compare small and mid-range laptops side by side. You may not see much physical difference in size.

Don't forget

A lot of the weight in a laptop is taken up by peripherals such as DVD writers, card readers and web-cams. The more of these that a laptop has the heavier it is likely to be.

Laptop jargon explained

Since laptops are essentially portable computers, a lot of the jargon is the same as for a desktop computer. However, it is worth looking at some of this jargon and the significance it has in terms of laptops.

- Processor. Also known as the central processing unit, or CPU, this refers to the processing of digital data as it is provided by programs on the computer. The more powerful the processor, the quicker the data is interpreted

- Memory. This closely relates to the processor and is also known as random-access memory, or RAM. Essentially, this type of memory manages the programs that are being run and the commands that are being executed. The greater the amount of memory there is, the quicker programs will run. With more RAM they will also be more stable and less likely to crash. In the current range of laptops, memory is measured in megabytes (Mb) or gigabytes (Gb)

- Storage. This refers to the amount of digital information that the laptop can store. In the current range of laptops storage is measured in gigabytes. There are no external signs of processor or memory on a laptop but the details are available from within the Computer option, which is accessed from the Start button (see Chapter 2 for details about the Start button)

Hard Disk Drives (2)

OS (C:)

70.3 GB free of 99.7 GB

Memory can be thought of as a temporary storage device as it only keeps information about the currently-open programs. Storage is more permanent as it keeps the information even when the laptop has been turned off.

- Optical drive. This is a drive on the laptop that is capable of reading information from, and copying it onto, a disc such as a CD or a DVD. Most modern laptops have internal optical drives such as CD writers or DVD writers

- Connectivity. This refers to the different types of media device to which the laptop can be connected. These include card readers for cards from digital cameras, USB devices such as music players and FireWire devices such as digital video cameras

- Graphics card. This is a device that enables images, video and animations to be displayed on the laptop. It is also sometimes known as a video card. The faster the graphics card, the better the quality the relevant media will be displayed at. In general, very fast graphics cards are really only needed for intensive multimedia applications such as video games or videos

- Wireless. This refers to a laptop's ability to connect wirelessly to a network, i.e. another computer or an Internet connection. In order to be able to do this, the laptop must have a wireless card, which enables it to connect to a network or high-speed Internet connection

- Ports. These are the parts of a laptop into which external devices can be plugged, using a cable such as a USB or a FireWire. They are usually located on the side of the laptop and there can be two or three of each

- Pointing device. This is the part of the laptop that replaces the traditional mouse as a means of moving the cursor on the screen. Most pointing devices are in the form of a touch pad, where a finger on a pad is used to move the cursor. An external mouse can also be connected to a laptop and used in the conventional way

- Web-cam. This is a type of camera that is fitted into the laptop and can be used to take stills photographs or communicate via video with other people

Hot tip

External optical drives can also be connected to a laptop through a USB cable.

Don't forget

For more on using wireless technology see Chapter 9.

Don't forget

USB stands for Universal Serial Bus and is a popular way of connecting external devices to computers.

13

Size and weight

The issues of size and weight are integral to the decision to buy a laptop. In addition to getting a machine with enough computing power it is also important to ensure that the screen is large enough for your needs and that it is light enough for you to carry around comfortably.

Size

The main issue with the size of a laptop is the dimension of the screen. This is usually measured in inches, diagonally from corner to corner. The range for the majority of laptops currently on the market is approximately 12–15 inches, with some more powerful models going up to 17 inches and above. When compared side by side, a 15-inch and a 12-inch model look like this:

When considering the size of screen it is important to think about how you are going to use your laptop:

- If you are going to use it mainly for functions such as letter writing and sending email then a smaller screen might suffice

- If you are going to use it mainly for functions such as surfing the Web or editing and looking at photographs then you may feel more comfortable with a larger screen

Weight

Unless you are buying a laptop to replace a desktop, weight should not be too much of an issue as most models are similar in this respect. However, make sure you physically feel the laptop before you buy it.

Beware

Looking at material on a smaller screen can be more tiring on the eyes as, by default, it is displayed proportionally smaller than on a larger screen. It is possible to change the size of the screen display, but this will lead to less material being displayed on the screen. See Chapter 2 to see how to change the screen display size.

Getting comfortable

Since you will probably be using your laptop in more than one location, the issue of finding a comfortable working position can be a vital one, particularly as you cannot put the keyboard and monitor in different positions as you can with a desktop computer. Whenever you are using your laptop try and make sure that you are sitting in a comfortable position, with your back well supported, and that the laptop is in a position where you can reach the keyboard easily and also see the screen without straining.

Despite the possible temptation to do so, avoid using your laptop in bed, on your lap or where you have to slouch or strain to reach the laptop properly:

Don't forget

Working comfortably at a laptop involves a combination of a good chair, good posture and good positioning of the laptop.

Hot tip

If possible, the best place to work at a laptop is at a dedicated desk or workstation.

15

Seating position

The ideal way to sit at a laptop is with an office-type chair that offers good support for your back. Even with these types of chairs it is important to maintain a good body position so that your back is straight and your head is pointing forwards.

If you do not have an office-type chair, use a chair with a straight back and place a cushion behind you for extra support and comfort as required.

Hot tip

One of the advantages of office-type chairs is that the height can usually be adjusted, and this can be a great help in achieving a comfortable position.

...cont'd

Laptop position

When working at your laptop it is important to have it positioned so that both the keyboard and the screen are in a comfortable position. If the keyboard is too low then you will have to slouch or strain to reach it:

If the keyboard is too high, your arms will be stretching. This could lead to pain in your tendons:

The ideal setup is to have the laptop in a position where you can sit with your forearms and wrists as level as possible while you are typing on the keyboard:

Beware

Take regular breaks when working with a laptop and stop working if you experience aches, or pins and needles in your arms or legs.

Adjusting the screen

Another factor in working comfortably at a laptop is the position of the screen. Unlike with a desktop computer, it is not feasible to have a laptop screen at eye level, as this would result in the keyboard being in too high a position. Instead, once you have achieved a comfortable seating position, open the screen so that it is approximately 90 degrees from your eye line:

One problem with laptop screens is that they can reflect glare from sunlight or indoor lighting:

If this happens, either change your position, or block out the light source using some form of blind or shade. Avoid squinting at a screen that is reflecting glare as this will quickly give you a headache.

Don't forget

Find a comfortable body position and adjust your laptop's position to this, rather than vice versa.

Beware

Most modern laptops have screens with an anti-glare coating. However, even this will not be very effective against bright sunlight that is shining directly onto the screen.

Carrying a laptop

As laptops are designed for mobility, it is safe to assume that they will have to be carried around at some point. Because of the weight of even the lightest laptops, it can be uncomfortable to carry a laptop for any length of time. To try and minimize this, it is important to follow a few rules:

- Carry the laptop with a carry case that is designed for this task

- Carry the laptop on one side of your body and move it from side to side if necessary

- Do not cross the strap over your shoulders and try not to carry too many other items at the same time

If you are travelling with your laptop you might be able to incorporate it into you luggage, particularly if it can be moved on wheels.

Beware

If you are carrying your laptop for any length of time make sure that you take regular breaks, otherwise you may cause yourself a strain or an injury.

Beware

If you place your laptop with another piece of luggage, make sure that you keep it with you at all times, so as to minimize the chance of theft.

Keyboard and mouse

Laptops have the same basic data input devices as desktop computers, i.e. a keyboard and a mouse. A laptop keyboard is very similar to a desktop one, although it is best to try the action of the keys before you buy a particular laptop, to ensure that they are not too "soft", i.e. that there is enough resistance when they are pressed.

One of the main differences between a laptop and a desktop computer is the mouse (or pointing device) that controls the on-screen cursor. In the early days of laptops, some of them had a small control stick to move the cursor. However, these have almost universally been replaced by touch pads, which are small, sensitive, square or rectangular pads that are activated by stroking a finger over them to move the cursor. It sometimes takes a bit of practice to get used to them but after a little experience they can be as effective as a traditional mouse. When using a keyboard or touch pad, avoid having your fingers too high:

Don't forget

Another method of moving the cursor is a track ball, which is a small, in-built, sphere that can be rolled with a finger to move the cursor.

19

Instead, keep your hands and fingers as flat as possible over the keyboard and the touch pad:

Using an external mouse

Not everyone likes touch pads or track balls as a means of moving the cursor on a laptop and it is true they can sometimes be slightly fiddly and prone to erratic movement if the control is too jerky. The good news is that it is perfectly possible to use a conventional mouse with a laptop to move the cursor.

A mouse can be connected to a laptop via one of the suitable sockets (ports) at the back of the laptop. These are usually in the form of a round serial port:

Once the mouse has been connected to the laptop it can be used in exactly the same way as with a desktop computer. In some cases it is possible to add a wireless mouse, which can be used without the need for a cable:

Don't forget

It is certainly worth perservering with a laptop's touch pad or track ball, even if it seems very frustrating at first. Once you have found the correct pressure to apply, it will become a lot easier to control.

Don't forget

Most laptops currently on the market can have a mouse attached via a USB port as well as a serial one, depending on the type of mouse.

Ports and slots

Most laptops have a slightly bewildering array of sockets and slots for connecting external devices. The sockets are known as ports, and these come in a variety of shapes for different devices:

- Parallel ports. These are used mainly for connecting printers. However, it is becoming a less frequently used method of connection and a lot of devices that previously used parallel ports now use USB (see below)

- Serial ports. These are used mainly for connecting an external mouse or even a keyboard

- USB. This is a method for connecting a variety of external devices such as digital cameras, MP3 music players, scanners and printers

- FireWire. This is a similar method of data transfer to USB but it is much faster. For this reason it is generally used for devices that need to transfer larger amounts of data, such as digital video cameras

The slots that are provided with laptops, and usually appear at the side, come in two main types:

- CD/DVD players or re-writers

- Expansion slots. These are empty compartments that can have various types of expansion cards fitted into them to give the laptop increased functionality. These can include video cards, sound cards and wireless network cards to enable the laptop to connect to a network without the need for a cable connection

Don't forget

An expansion card is a solid board that contains circuits with the information needed for the required task. The expansion card can then communicate with the laptop's operating system.

The wonder of wireless

For anyone who has struggled with a tangle of computer cables and wires, the advent of wireless technology has been one of the great computer breakthroughs of recent years.

Wireless technology does exactly what the name suggests: it allows a wireless-enabled computer to communicate with other similarly enabled devices, such as other computers, printers or an Internet connection. First of all the devices have to be set up as a network, i.e. they have to be linked together so that they know they should be communicating with each other. Once this has been done, files can be shared or sent to the printer, and the Internet browsed, all without the need to connect the devices using a cable.

In order to be part of a wireless network, a laptop has to have a wireless capability. Most modern laptops come with wireless cards already installed; otherwise, they can be installed in any available expansion slot.

Hotspots

One of the great growth areas of wireless technology is hotspots. These are public areas that have been set up to wirelessly distribute the Internet. This means that anyone with a wireless card in their laptop can, if they are within a certain range, access the Internet in a variety of public places. These include:

- Coffee shops
- Airports
- Hotels
- Libraries
- Supermarkets

Hotspots operate using Wi-Fi technology, which is the method by which the signal from the network is transferred to individual users. Most hotspots have a limited range of approximately 100 yards. Some are free to use, while others charge a fee, depending on usage.

Beware

One concern about hotspots is security. This is because if you can wirelessly access a network, someone else could then also access your laptop and data. A lot of hotspots have software in place to try and stop this.

Don't forget

For more information on hotspots, Wi-Fi and wireless networks, see Chapter 9.

Cleaning a laptop

Like most things, laptops benefit greatly from a little care and attention. The two most important areas to keep clean are the screen and the keyboard.

Cleaning the screen

All computer screens quickly collect dust and fingerprints, and laptops are no different. If this is left too long it can make the screen harder to read and cause eye strain and headaches. Clean the screen regularly with the following cleaning materials:

- A lint-free cloth, similar to the type used to clean camera lenses (it is important not to scratch the screen in any way)

- An alcohol-free cleaning fluid that is recommended for computer screens

- Screen wipes, again that are recommended for use on computer screens

Cleaning the keyboard

Keyboards are notorious for accumulating dust, fluff and crumbs. One way to solve this problem is to turn the laptop upside down and very gently shake it to loosen any foreign objects. Failing this, a can of condensed air can be used with a narrow nozzle to blow out any stubborn items that remain lodged in the keys.

Don't forget

The outer casing of a laptop can be cleaned with the same fluid as used for the screen. Equally effective can be a duster or a damp (but not wet) cloth and warm water. Keep soap away from laptops if possible.

23

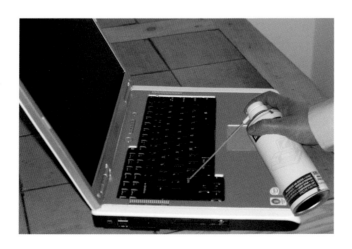

Choosing a carry case

When you are transporting your laptop it could be placed in any convenient bag, such as a backpack, a duffle bag or even a large handbag. However, there are several advantages to using a proper laptop carry case:

- It will probably be more comfortable when you are carrying it as it is designed specifically for this job

- The laptop will be more secure as it should fit properly in the case

- You should be able to keep all of your laptop accessories in one case

Beware

A laptop case should also be lockable, either with its own internal lock, or with a fastening through which a padlock can be put.

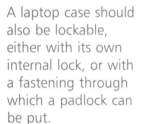

When choosing a carry case, look for one that fits your laptop well and has a strap to keep it secure inside:

Also, make sure that there are enough additional spaces and pockets for accessories, such as cables and an external mouse. Finally, choosing a case with a padded shoulder strap will be of a considerable benefit if you have to carry your laptop for any length of time.

Spares and accessories

Whenever you are going anywhere with your laptop there are always spares and accessories to consider. Some of these are just nice things to have, while others could be essential to ensure that you can still use your laptop if anything goes wrong while you are on your travels. Items to consider for putting in your laptop case include:

- Spare battery. This is probably the most important spare if you are going to be away from home for any length of time, and particularly if you think you may be unable to access a power supply for a period of time, and so be unable to charge your laptop battery. Like all batteries, laptop batteries slowly lose power over time and do not keep their charge for as long as when they are new. It is a good idea to always keep an eye on how much battery power you have left and, if you are running low, to try and conserve as much energy as possible. Although laptop batteries are bulky and heavy, this could mean the difference between frustration and relief, if you are left with no battery power

- Power cable. This is the cable that can be used to power the laptop when it is not being run on battery power. It usually consists of a cable and a power adapter, which makes it rather bulky and heavy. Whenever possible this should be used rather than the internal battery, and it should be kept with the laptop at all times

Don't forget

For more information on batteries see Chapter 3.

...cont'd

- External mouse. This can be used instead of the laptop's touch pad or track ball. Some people prefer a traditional mouse, particularly if they are going to be working on their laptop for an extended period of time

- Multi-card reader. This is a device that can be used to copy data from the cards used in digital cameras. If you have a digital camera, it is possible to download the photographs from it directly onto a laptop with a cable. However, a multi-card reader can be more efficient and it also enables you to download photographs from other people's cameras, even if they have different types of cards from your own camera's

- Headphones. These can be used to listen to music or films if you are in the company of other people and you do not want to disturb them. They can also be very useful if there are distracting noises from other people

- Pen drive. This is a small device that can be used to copy data to and from your laptop. It connects via a USB port and is about the size of a packet of chewing gum. It is an excellent way of backing up files from your laptop when you are away from home

- Cleaning material. The materials described on page 23 can be taken to ensure your laptop is always in tip-top condition for use

- DVDs/CDs. Video or music DVDs and CDs can be taken to provide mobile entertainment, and blank ones can be taken to copy data onto, similarly to using a pen drive

Hot tip

It is important that headphones are comfortable to wear for an extended period of time. In general, the types that fit over the ears are more comfortable than the "bud" variety that are inserted into the ear.

Don't forget

Backing up is the process of copying folders and files from your laptop onto an external device, for safekeeping in case the folders and files on the laptop are deleted or corrupted.

2 Around a laptop

This chapter shows how to quickly get up and running with your laptop so that you can start to use it productively. It covers starting the laptop and customizing it to best suit your needs. It also looks at adding external devices to your laptop so that it can be used to cater for all of your computing needs.

Opening up

The first step towards getting started with a new laptop is to open it ready for use. The traditional clamshell design keeps the screen and keyboard together through the use of an internal clip or connector. This can be released by a button on the exterior of the laptop, which is usually positioned at the front or side. This can be activated by sliding or pressing, which releases the catch holding the screen:

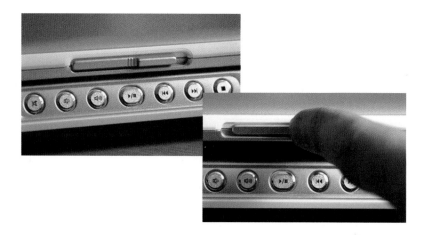

Once the screen has been released it can then be positioned ready for use. The screen should stay in any position in which it is placed:

Turning on

The button for turning on a laptop, ready for use, is usually located next to the keyboard:

The laptop can be turned on by pushing this button firmly. The laptop will then probably make a chime to indicate that it has been turned on and then begin loading the operating system (the software that is used to run and manage all of the laptop's programs, folders and files). Once the laptop has completed its startup procedure the opening screen should be displayed. At this point the laptop is ready for use.

Start button

The Start button is the point from which all of the functionality of your laptop can be accessed. This includes programs, folders, files, searching and important elements of the operating system such as the Control Panel. This is also where the options for shutting down the laptop can be accessed. The Start button is located at the bottom left corner of the screen:

Click once on the Start button to see a list of the available options. This is known as the Start Menu:

Don't forget

The examples here use Windows Vista, the latest version of the Windows operating system from Microsoft.

Don't forget

Logically enough, the Start Menu is a good place to begin investigating the contents of your laptop.

Don't forget

The Start button can also be used to access the controls for turning off your laptop and putting it into Sleep mode. See page 34 for more details.

Start Menu

The Start Menu has a number of options for accessing programs and elements within your laptop and also for searching for items on your system.

Opening programs

A list of recently used programs is shown on the Start Menu. Click once on a program to open it.

 Windows Photo Gallery

 Windows Update

 Windows Media Player

All Programs

To access all of the programs on your laptop:

1   Click on All Programs, or hold the cursor over the button for a couple of seconds

2   A list of your laptop's programs is shown here

 Windows Mail

Windows Media Center

Windows Media Player

Windows Meeting Space

Windows Movie Maker

Windows Photo Gallery

Don't forget

The All Programs function in Vista enables you to see all of the programs on your laptop on one menu, unlike in previous versions of Windows, which used a hierarchical structure.

...cont'd

Pinning programs

The list of recently used programs changes when new programs are opened and used. However, it is possible to pin your favorite programs to the Start Menu so that they are always accessible from the Start button. To do this:

1 Right-click on a program and select Pin to Start Menu

  Internet Explorer

Welcome Center

2 The program name is added above the line on the Start Menu, indicating it has been pinned there i.e. it will remain there permanently, or until it is removed

Using Quick Launch

The Quick Launch function is part of the Taskbar, located at the bottom of the screen next to the Start button. It displays currently-open programs and also favorite programs so that they can be accessed quickly without the need to use the Start Menu.

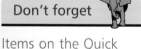
Items can be added to the Quick Launch bar from the Start Menu. To do this:

1 Right-click on a program and select Add to Quick Launch

2 The program icon is added to the Quick Launch bar

Searching

The Start Menu can be used to search for items on your laptop and also on the Internet. To do this:

1 Enter the keyword or phrase for which you want to search here

2 Click on "See all results" to view the search results within your overall file structure or the Internet

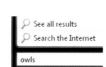

3 The results are shown here. Click on an item to view it

Don't forget

Click on the Search the Internet link to look for items just on the Internet rather than on your laptop.

Hot tip

The items on the Start Menu can be customized by right-clicking on the item name and selecting the Properties option.

33

Other items

The Start Menu can also be used to access other areas of your laptop such as the Computer or the Control Panel:

Shutting down and sleeping

Power management is an important issue with laptops, and so every opportunity should be taken to conserve power. One way in which this can be done is to turn the computer into low-power mode when it is not being used. This is called Sleep mode, which keeps the items on which you are working in the laptop's memory and puts it into a low-power mode. You can then quickly wake up the laptop and immediately resume your work from where you left it. The laptop can also be shut down from here.

To activate Sleep and Shut Down modes:

1 For Sleep mode, click here on the Start Menu, or

2 Click here on the Start Menu

3 Click on the Sleep button

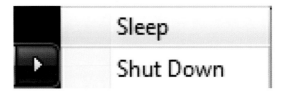

Don't forget

The same process can be used to restart the laptop. Clicking on Restart closes all programs, shuts down the laptop and then restarts it.

4 To shut down the laptop, click on the Shut Down button

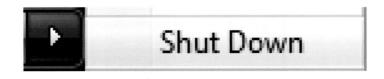

Mobility Center

Mobility is one of the key features of a laptop and within Windows Vista there is a Mobility Center for adjusting a variety of settings that can be used for a laptop. To access the Mobility Center:

1 Click on the Start button

2 Click on the Control Panel button

3 Click on the Mobile PC link

Mobile PC
Change battery settings
Adjust commonly used mobility settings

4 Click on the Windows Mobility Center link

Windows Mobility Center
Adjust commonly used mobility settings
Adjust screen brightness
Adjust settings before giving a presentation
Connect to a projector or other external display

5 The Windows Mobility Center contains options for items such as the display brightness, sound volume, battery settings, wireless connections, connecting an external monitor, synchronizing with other devices and connecting to a projector for slideshows or presentations

Don't forget

For more information about battery settings and usage, see Chapter 3.

35

Don't forget

Depending on the manufacturer of the laptop, there may be some additional options within the Mobility Center.

Adjusting screen resolution

When working with your laptop it is important to be able to see everything on the screen clearly and comfortably. It is possible to change the size at which everything is displayed on the screen by altering the screen resolution. To do this:

1 Click on the Start button

2 Click on the Control Panel button

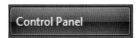

Some screen resolutions change the proportions of what is displayed on the screen. This can create the effect of items appearing squashed or unnatural.

3 Under the Appearance and Personalization section, click on the "Adjust screen resolution" link

Appearance and Personalization
Change desktop background
Customize colors
Adjust screen resolution

4 The Display Settings window contains options for altering the screen resolution

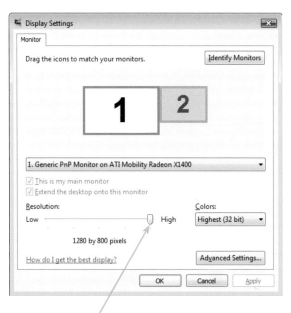

5 Drag this slider to alter the screen resolution

6   Click on the OK button to apply the new sreen resolution

> OK

7   Click on the Yes button if you want to keep the new settings

Display Settings

Do you want to keep these display settings?

> Yes   No

Reverting to previous display settings in 6 seconds.

Don't forget

Experiment with different screen resolutions to see which one you feel most comfortable with, particularly when using your laptop for a prolonged period.

37

8   Different resolution settings change the overall size of everything on the screen

Adjusting text

As well as changing the overall screen resolution, it is also possible to adjust the size at which text is displayed. To do this:

Don't forget

The Ease of Access Center also has options for using a Magnifier, to make parts of the screen appear larger, a Narrator, which reads on-screen text aloud, an On-Screen Keyboard that can be activated using the mouse and a High Contrast setting for the screen.

 Click on the Start button

 Click on the Control Panel button

Control Panel

Click on the Appearance and Personalization link

Appearance and Personalization
Change desktop background
Customize colors
Adjust screen resolution

 Click on the Ease of Access Center link

Ease of Access Center
Accommodate low vision | Change screen reader |
Underline keyboard shortcuts and access keys |
Turn High Contrast on or off

 The Ease of Access Center window has various options for viewing items more clearly

Explore all settings
When you select these settings, they will automatically start each time you log on.

Use the computer without a display
Optimize for blindness

Make the computer easier to see
Optimize visual display

Use the computer without a mouse or keyboard
Set up alternative input devices

6 Click on the "Make the computer easier to see" link

 Make the computer easier to see
Optimize visual display

7 Click on the "Change the size of text and icons" link

Make things on the screen larger

 Change the size of text and icons

8 Check on the "Larger scale" button

39

DPI Scaling

Choose a smaller scale to fit more information on the screen or a larger scale to make text more readable. How do I know which DPI to choose?

○ Default scale (96 DPI) - fit more information

◉ Larger scale (120 DPI) - make text more readable

9 Click on the OK button

OK

Adjusting volume

There are different sources of sounds on a laptop. The main two are:

- Sounds from the speakers
- System Windows sounds

The volume for each of these can be adjusted independently of the other. To do this:

1 Click on the Start button

2 Click on the Control Panel button

3 Click on the Hardware and Sound link
Hardware and Sound
Play CDs or other media automatically
Printer
Mouse

4 In the Sound section, click on the "Adjust system volume" link
Sound
Adjust system volume

5 In the Volume Mixer window, drag the sliders to adjust the volume for a particular item

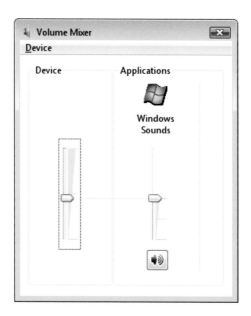

Loading CDs and DVDs

CDs and DVDs are an important aspect of life with a laptop. They can be used to store information and also for playing music or movies, particularly when traveling. To load CDs or DVDs:

1 Locate the CD or DVD drive. This will be a slot that is

located at the side or front of the laptop

2 Press the button on the front of the drive once to eject the tray

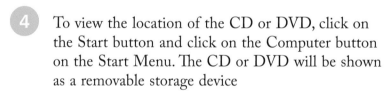

3 Insert the CD or DVD into the tray and press the button again to close it, or push it gently closed

Don't forget

For a music or video CD or DVD the appropriate program to play the disc should open up automatically when it is inserted. If not, access it as shown in Step 4 and double-click on the disc to open it.

4 To view the location of the CD or DVD, click on the Start button and click on the Computer button on the Start Menu. The CD or DVD will be shown as a removable storage device

Connecting a printer

At some point, most people working with a laptop will want to print out something, whether it is a photograph, a letter or an email. In order for this to be done, a printer has to be connected. This involves physically connecting the printer and also adding the software that is required for the printer to communicate with your laptop. To do this:

1 Connect the printer to the laptop using either a parallel port connection or a USB one, depending on the type of printer

Parallel port

USB port

42

2 Click on the Start button and click on the Control Panel button on the Start Menu

3 In the Hardware and Sound section, click on the Printer link

Hardware and Sound
Play CDs or other media automatically
Printer
Mouse

4 The Printers window shows which printers (if any) have already been added to the laptop

5 To add a new printer (only with a parallel port), click on the "Add a printer" button

6 Click on the "Add a local printer" box

7 Check on the "Use an existing port" button

8 Click on the Next button

9 The "Install the printer driver" section has options for installing a driver from the laptop or using the disc that came with the printer. If you have the disc click on the Have Disk button

Have Disk...

10 Insert the disc and click on the OK button

11 Once the drivers have been installed the printer is ready for use

43

Scanners and cameras

Two other popular devices to use with a laptop are a scanner and a digital camera. These can both be connected to a laptop in a similar way as with a printer, although in a lot of cases, the operating system (Vista) will recognize the scanner or digital camera and take you through the installation process for the necessary software (drivers). To connect a scanner or digital camera:

44

1 Connect the scanner or digital camera to the laptop using the USB cable

2 Click on the "Locate and install driver software (recommended)" link

3 Vista searches for the necessary drivers for the camera or scanner

4 Vista starts to download the necessary drivers

5 Once the drivers have been installed, a window like this is displayed

6 Click on the Close button

Adding software manually

If the software for your camera or scanner is not downloaded and installed automatically, it can be added manually, using the CD that would have come with the device. To do this:

1 Click on the Start button

2 Click on the Control Panel button

3 Click on the Hardware and Sound link

4 Click on the Scanners and Cameras link

5 The names of any existing devices are shown here

Don't forget

Installed scanner and digital-camera software should appear on the All Programs list, which can be accessed from the Start Menu.

45

6 Click on the Add Device button to add a new camera or scanner

7 The Scanner and Camera Installation Wizard takes you through the process of adding the new device, including adding the necessary software

Pen drives

Pen drives are small devices that can be used for copying files and then transferring them between computers. In some ways they are the natural successor to floppy discs. To connect a pen drive to a laptop and use it:

1 Connect the pen drive to one of the laptop's USB ports

2 The pen drive should be recognized automatically and the necessary software installed so that it is ready to use

3 Click on the Start button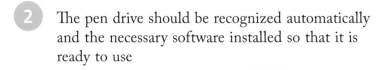

4 Click on the Computer button on the Start Menu

5 The pen drive should appear under the Devices with Removable Storage section

6 Double-click on the pen drive to view its contents. The files can then be used in the same way as any others on your laptop

3 Battery issues

Battery power is crucial to a laptop and this chapter shows how to get the best performance from your battery, look after it and deal with any problems.

Types of battery

A laptop's battery is one of the items that helps to define its identity: without it the portable nature of the laptop would be very different as it would always have to be connected with a power cable. Laptops have used a variety of different types of batteries since they were first produced and over the years these have become smaller, lighter and more powerful. However, laptop batteries are still relatively heavy and bulky and are one of the major sources of weight in the machine:

Don't forget

The type of battery provided with a laptop, and the approximate lifespan for each charge, should be displayed with the details about the machine on the manufacturer's website or in the promotional literature that comes with it.

The types of batteries used in modern laptops are:

- Lithium-ion. This is a type of battery that has a good weight-to-power ratio and loses its charge at a relatively slow rate. However, they can be prone to overheating if they are not treated properly or are defective

- Lithium polymer. This is an advanced version of the lithium-ion battery. It is generally considered to be a more stable design

These types of batteries are rechargeable and so they can be used numerous times once they initially run out. However, all rechargeable batteries eventually wear out and have to be replaced.

Power consumption

Battery life for each charge of laptop batteries is one area on which engineers have worked very hard since laptops were first introduced. For most modern laptops the average battery life for each charge is approximately between three and five hours. However, this is dependent on the power consumption of the laptop, i.e. how much power is being used to perform particular tasks. Power-intensive tasks will reduce the battery life of each charge cycle. These types of tasks include:

- Watching a DVD

- Editing digital video

- Editing digital photographs

- Listening to music

When you are using your laptop you can always monitor how much battery power you currently have available. This is shown by the battery icon that appears at the bottom right on the Taskbar:

Because of the vital role that the battery plays in relation to your laptop it is important to try and conserve its power as much as possible. To do this:

- Where possible, use the mains adapter rather than the battery when using your laptop

- Use the Sleep function when you are not actively using your laptop (see Chapter 2)

- Use power-management functions to save battery power (see next pages)

Beware

If you are undertaking an energy-intensive task, such as watching a DVD, try and use the external AC/DC power cable rather than the battery. Otherwise the battery may drain very quickly and the laptop close down.

Battery management

Unlike desktop computers, laptops have additional options for how the battery is managed. These allow you to set things like individual power schemes for the battery and to view how much charge is left in the battery. This can be done from the Control Panel. To access the options for managing your laptop's battery:

Don't forget

A power scheme can be set for the battery in the same way as for an external power source and different settings can be applied.

50

1 Click on the Start button

2 Click on the Control Panel button

3 Click on the Hardware and Sound link

Hardware and Sound
Play CDs or other media automatically
Printer
Mouse

4 Click on Power Options

Power Options
Change battery settings | Change what the power buttons do |
Require a password when the computer wakes |
Change when the computer sleeps

Power Plans

The Power Options window displays the available settings for balancing battery usage and your laptop's performance. Click on the buttons to change to a different power plan:

...cont'd

System Settings

Within the Power Options window it is possible to select settings for how the laptop operates when the power or the sleep button is pressed, or when the lid is closed. To do this:

1 In the Power Options window, click on one of these links

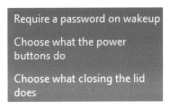

2 The options are displayed in System Settings

Beware

If you don't protect your laptop with a password for when it is woken from sleep, anyone could access your folders and files if they wake the laptop from sleep.

51

3 Click here to select a behavior for a certain action, either

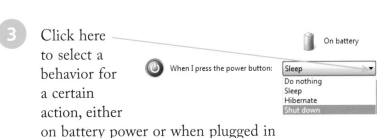

on battery power or when plugged in

4 Check on the "Require a password (recommended)" button to specify the use of a password to access the laptop when it wakes up after being put to sleep

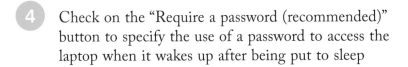

...cont'd

Editing plan settings
To edit the settings for a specific power plan:

1 Click on one of these options in the Power Options window

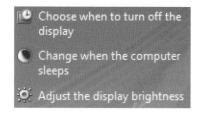

52

2 Select options for turning off the display when the laptop is not being used and when the computer goes to sleep, and also the display brightness, either on battery power or when the laptop is plugged in

Power Meter
To access the Power Meter to view how the battery is performing:

1 Click on the Battery Meter link in the Power Options window

2 The Power Meter displays the current charge of the battery and the Battery Health tab contains details about how the battery is performing

Charging the battery

Laptop batteries are charged using an AC/DC adapter, which can also be used to power the laptop instead of the battery. If the laptop is turned on and being powered by the AC/DC adapter, the battery will be charged at the same time, although at a slower rate than if it is being charged with the laptop turned off.

The AC/DC adapter should be supplied with a new laptop and consists of a cable and a power adapter. To charge a laptop battery using an AC/DC adapter:

Don't forget

A laptop battery can be charged whether the laptop is turned on or off.

1. Connect the AC/DC adapter and the cable and plug it into the mains socket

2. Attach the AC/DC adapter to the laptop and turn on at the mains socket

3. When the laptop is turned on the Power Meter icon is visible at the bottom right of the Taskbar. Double-click on this to view the current power details

Removing the battery

Although a laptop's battery does not have to be removed on a regular basis, there may be occasions when you want to do this. These include:

- If the laptop freezes, i.e. you are unable to undertake any operations using the keyboard or mouse and you cannot turn off the laptop using the power button

- If you are traveling, particularly in extreme temperatures. In situations such as this you may prefer to keep the battery with you to try and avoid exposing it to either very hot or very cold temperatures

To remove a laptop battery:

Don't forget

To re-insert the battery, or a new battery, push it gently into the battery compartment until it clicks firmly into place.

1 With the laptop turned off and the lid closed, turn the laptop upside down

2 Locate the battery compartment and either push or slide the lock that keeps the battery in place

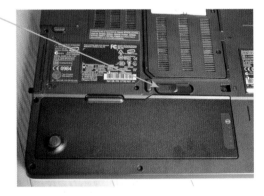

3 Slide the battery out of its compartment

Dead and spare batteries

No energy source lasts forever and laptop batteries are no exception to this rule. Over time, the battery will operate less efficiently until it will not be possible to charge the battery at all. With average usage, most laptop batteries should last approximately five years, although they will start to lose performance before this. Some signs of a dead laptop battery are if:

- Nothing happens when the laptop is turned on using just battery power

- The laptop shuts down immediately if it is being run on the AC/DC adapter and the cord is suddenly removed

- The Battery Meter shows no movement when the AC/DC adapter is connected, i.e. the Battery Meter remains at 1%

Spare battery

Because of the limited lifespan of laptop batteries it is worth considering buying a spare battery. Although these are not cheap it can be a valuable investment, particularly if you spend a lot of time traveling with your laptop and you are not always near a source of mains electricity. In situations such as this a spare battery could enable you to keep using your laptop if your original battery runs out of power.

When buying a spare battery, check with the laptop's manufacturer that it will be compatible: in most cases the manufacturer will also be able to supply you with a spare battery for your laptop.

Battery troubleshooting

If you look after your laptop battery well it should provide you with several years of mobile computing power. However, there are some problems that may occur with the battery:

- It won't keep its charge even when connected to an AC/DC adapter. The battery is probably flat and should be replaced

- It only charges up a limited amount. Over time, laptop batteries become less efficient and so do not hold their charge so well. One way to try and improve this is to drain the battery completely before it is charged again

- It keeps its charge but runs down quickly. This can be caused by the use of a lot of power-hungry applications on the laptop. The more work the laptop has to do to run applications, such as those involving videos or games, the more power will be required from the battery and the faster it will run down

- It is fully charged but does not appear to work at all when inserted. Check that the battery has clicked into place properly in the battery compartment and that the battery and laptop terminals are clean and free from dust or moisture

- It is inserted correctly but still does not work. The battery may have become damaged in some way, such as becoming very wet. If you know the battery is damaged in any way, do not insert it, as it could short-circuit the laptop. If the battery has been in contact with liquid, dry it out completely before you try inserting it into the laptop. If it is thoroughly dry it may work again

- It gets very hot when in operation. This could be caused by a faulty battery and it can be dangerous and lead to a fire. If in doubt, turn off the laptop immediately and consult the manufacturer. In some cases, faulty laptop batteries are recalled, so keep an eye on the manufacturer's website to see if there are any details of this if you are concerned

Don't forget

If there is no response from your laptop when you turn it on in battery mode, try removing the battery and re-inserting it. If there is still no response then the battery is probably flat and should be replaced.

Hot tip

If you are not going to be using your laptop for an extended period of time, remove the battery and store it in a safe, dry, cool place.

4 Laptop software

Software is essential to the overall operation of a laptop and also for any activity that you want to do on it. This chapter contains an overview of the latest Windows operating system (Vista) and how to use the system software to perform tasks such as managing photos and enjoying music.

Around Windows Vista

Windows Vista is the latest computer operating system from Microsoft and it is installed on most new IBM-compatible laptops, i.e. all of those that are not produced by Apple. These account for over 90% of the laptop market, which means that a lot of people are going to be looking at Vista.

For most Vista users there are two main interfaces:

- Basic, which can be used on computers that do not have enough power to run the more advanced version of Vista. The Basic interface comes with the Vista Home Basic version of the operating system

- Aero, which provides a more dynamic and powerful interface to improve the user experience

Desktop

When your laptop is first turned on you will see the Vista desktop. This contains similar elements for both the Basic and the Aero interfaces:

Don't forget

In total there are four different versions of Vista. These are Home Basic, Home Premium, Business, and Ultimate. Apart from Home Basic they all have the Aero interface, and for most home users Home Premium would be the best option, as long as their computer is powerful enough.

Shortcuts   Desktop area

Start button   Taskbar

Aero experience

Aero, the new interface with Vista Home Premium and above, provides a number of graphical features that can make it easier, and more pleasurable, to navigate around your workspace, folders and files.

Glass

In previous versions of Windows all of the open windows were solid. However, Aero has a function where the borders of all windows are translucent. This creates a more integrated appearance and it also enables you to see more of the window behind the one on which you are currently working.

Hot tip

The appearance of the glass effect can be customized in the Control Panel. To do this, click on the Start button, select the Control Panel and select Appearance and Personalization> Window Color and Appearance, and then select a new style for the glass effect.

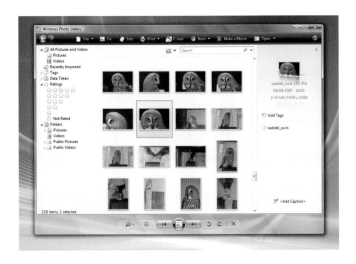

...cont'd

Flip

Another innovation in Aero is the Flip function. This is operated by pressing the Alt+Tab keys at the same time. This displays real-time thumbnails (which update as the program is working) of the programs you have running:

You can tab through the thumbnails:

When you stop at one and release the Alt key, that program becomes the active one, i.e it comes to the front, ready for use, with the others behind it:

Don't forget

In addition to the Flip function showing real-time thumbnails, the Taskbar (along the bottom of the screen) also shows real-time icons: if a program is performing a task, this can be viewed by moving the cursor over the program icon located on the Taskbar.

Flip 3D

A further development of the flip idea in Aero is the Flip 3D function. This is accessed by pressing the Windows key on your keyboard and the Tab key at the same time. This displays all of the open windows in a 3D stacked effect:

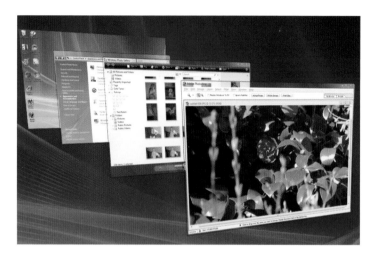

61

To move through the stacked windows, keep the Windows key held down and press the Tab key to change the order of the stacked windows:

Using Vista Basic

Despite the rich graphical appearance of Aero, it is not to everyone's taste. The glass effect, in particular, can be slightly distracting as it does not show enough of the screen behind for it to be clear and results in a rather fuzzy combination. However, even if you have a version of Vista that uses Aero, it is still possible to change this so that the more traditional Basic color scheme and appearance can be used. To do this:

 Click on the Start button

 Click on the Control Panel button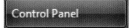

3 Click on the Appearance and Personalization link

Appearance and Personalization

Change desktop background
Change the color scheme
Adjust screen resolution

4 Click on the Personalization link

Personalization

Change desktop background | Change the color scheme
Adjust screen resolution | Change screen saver | Change the theme

5 Click on the Window Color and Appearance link

 ### Window Color and Appearance

Fine tune the color and style of your windows.

6 The Appearance Settings window has options for how the windows will appear for different color schemes

7 Under "Color scheme" select Windows Vista Basic

8 Click on the OK button

9 Vista Basic provides a cleaner and more traditional appearance for the windows

Don't forget

For a lot of people, the Vista Basic interface is better to work with, particularly over a long period of time.

Welcome Center

The Welcome Center in Vista is an area to help users get started with Vista and get it looking the way they want, and to give them access to items such as software updates and security services. When you first open Vista, i.e. when you first turn on your laptop, the Welcome Center will be displayed by default:

Check this box to always display the Welcome Center when you start up your laptop

Click on an item in the Welcome Center. A summary of it is displayed at the top of the window. Click on the "Show more details" link to access the full function:

The main items in the Welcome Center are shown at the top of the window. By default, there are 14 and it is possible to view them all at the same time. To do this:

1 Click on the "Show all 14 items" link to view the full range of options for the Welcome Center items

1. Get started with Windows (14)

 View computer details

 Windows Anytime Upgrade

Show all 14 items...

These include:

- *View computer details.* This displays details of your system, such as the version of Vista being used, the processor and the amount of memory

- *Transfer files and settings.* This can be used to transfer items from one computer to another, but they have to be networked together

- *Add new users.* This can be used to set up specific user accounts for individual people

- *Windows Anytime Upgrade.* This enables you to upgrade your version of Windows Vista. This is done through an online service and requires an active connection to the Internet

...cont'd

● *Connect to the Internet.* This is a Wizard that takes you through the steps for connecting to the Internet

● *What's new in Windows Vista.* This is an online service that gives an overview of the latest Vista functions

● *Personalize Windows.* This takes you directly to the Personalization section of the Control Panel

● *Register Windows online.* This can be used to register your copy of Vista so that you are eligible for upgrades and news about the product

● *Windows Media Center.* This opens up the Media Center for viewing multimedia such as photos, video and TV and listening to music

● *Windows Basics.* This is an online service that gives a simple overview of working with Windows

● *Ease of Access Center.* This takes you directly to the Ease of Access Center section of the Control Panel

● *Back Up and Restore Center.* This takes you directly to the Back Up and Restore section of the Control Panel, which is used to back up your folders and files

● *Windows Vista Demos.* These are videos that show you how to perform certain functions with Vista

● *Control Panel.* This takes you directly to the Control Panel, from where numerous options can be selected

Don't forget

A lot of the options in the Welcome Center, such as the Ease of Access Center and the Back Up and Restore Center, can also be accessed from within the Control Panel.

Sidebar and gadgets

The Sidebar in Vista is a function that enables you to display a range of small programs known as gadgets. These cover a variety of everyday topics, such as weather forecasts, a clock, a calendar and up-to-the-minute news feeds. Gadgets can be added to, or removed from, the Sidebar. The Sidebar itself can also be customized. To display the Sidebar:

1 Click on the Start button and click on the Windows Sidebar button on the Start Menu; or

2 Click on the Start button and select All Programs>Accessories>Windows Sidebar

By default, the Sidebar is displayed at the right-hand side of the screen:

Hot tip

The Sidebar can be closed by right-clicking on it and selecting Close Sidebar.

67

...cont'd

Adding gadgets

There are a number of gadgets that are provided with Vista and these can be added to the Sidebar. To do this:

Hot tip

Gadgets can also be accessed for adding to the Sidebar by right-clicking on the Sidebar and selecting Add Gadgets.

1 Click here at the top of the Sidebar

2 The range of available gadgets is displayed in a new window

3 Double-click on a gadget to add it to the Sidebar

Customizing a gadget

The way individual gadgets operate can be customized to meet individual needs. To do this:

Hot tip

Gadgets can also be added to the Sidebar from the Gadgets window by dragging them directly onto the Sidebar.

1 Click once on a gadget, or move the cursor over it, and click here to access its properties

2 Select the required properties for the gadget

3 Click on the OK button

Customizing the Sidebar

The functionality of the Sidebar can also be customized. To do this:

1 Click on the Start button and select the Control Panel button

2 Click on the Appearance and Personalization link

Appearance and Personalization

3 Click on the Windows Sidebar Properties link

Windows Sidebar Properties
Add gadgets to Sidebar
Choose whether to keep Sidebar on top of other windows

4 The Windows Sidebar Properties window contains options for customizing the Sidebar

5 Check this box if you want the Sidebar to appear every time you turn on your laptop

6 Check this box if you want the Sidebar to be visible all of the time, i.e. on top of any other open windows

7 Select an option for whether you want the Sidebar to appear on the left or right of the screen

8 Click on the OK button

Hot tip

The properties for the Sidebar can also be accessed by right-clicking on the Sidebar and selecting Properties.

69

Windows Media Center

The Windows Media Center is incorporated into Vista and it provides one location for viewing, and listening to, a variety of multimedia content. This includes DVDs, home movies, downloaded TV programs, music and photographs. To access Windows Media Center:

1. Click on the Start button and click on the Windows Media Center button on the Start Menu; or

2. Click on the Start button and select All Programs> Windows Media Center

3. When the Media Center is first accessed you will be asked some questions about your laptop's Internet and network capabilities. Click on the Next button to complete the process

4. Once the questions have been answered, the Media Center is ready for use

Using Windows Media Center

To use the Media Center to view multimedia content:

1 Click on one of the options to view a type of media

2 Select a location where the media is situated

Don't forget

For more information about Windows Media Center, have a look at "Windows Vista Media Center in Easy Steps" in this series.

71

3 Click here to play the selected media as a slide show

4 Use these controls to navigate through the media

Windows Media Player

The Windows Media Player is similar to the Media Center in some ways, although its main focus is playing digital content such as music or videos.

Hot tip

The Media Player can also be used to copy music onto blank CDs.

To access Windows Media Center:

1 Click on the Start button and click on the Windows Media Player button on the Start Menu; or

2 Click on the Start button and select All Programs> Windows Media Player

Windows Media Player

3 The Windows Media Player has an interface that makes it possible to organize your music and videos and create your own playlists

Don't forget

For more information on using the Windows Media Player to play music see pages 80–81 in this chapter.

Writing a letter

Word processing is one of the most common activities for any computer user. This can include the production of a complex report, or a family letter. When using a laptop with Vista, word processing can be done with Microsoft Word, but if you want to do fairly straightforward word processing, such as letter writing, there is a built-in word processor that comes with Vista. This is called WordPad. To access it:

1 Click on the Start button and select All Programs> Accessories>WordPad

 WordPad

2 WordPad provides basic word processing in a clear interface

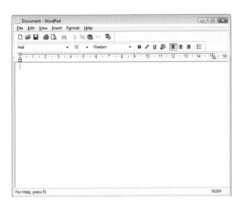

3 Use these options to select font type and size

| Arial | ▼ | 10 | ▼ |

4 Use these buttons to add bold, italics, underlining, text color, alignment and bullet points

Don't forget

Microsoft Word comes as part of the Microsoft Office package of programs, which also includes Excel and PowerPoint. If you want to use these it is usually cheaper to buy Office as part of a package when you buy your laptop, rather than separately.

Creating a spreadsheet

Spreadsheets can be a daunting prospect but they are essentially a way to list and sort data, with the option of including calculations. They can be used for anything from complex financial documents, to a list of your CDs or a means of working out your household expenses.

The most widely used spreadsheet software is Microsoft Excel, which comes with the Office suite of programs. Once this has been loaded the Excel button should be visible on the Start Menu or the Taskbar. To use Excel:

Don't forget

If the Excel button is not visible on either the Start Menu or the Taskbar, click on the Start button and the All Programs button. Select Microsoft Excel.

1 Click on this button on the Start Menu or the Taskbar

2 Spreadsheets are formatted into rows and columns. Rows are identified by numbers and columns by letters. Each box is known as a cell

3 A toolbar and menu bar are situated at the top of the spreadsheet. These are used to add and format data in the spreadsheet

Hot tip

The names of workbooks can be edited by double-clicking on the existing name and over-typing it. This way workbooks can be created for related topics, such as household expenses and vacation expenses.

4 Click here to open a new spreadsheet

New

5 Different workbooks can be used within the same spreadsheet. Click on these tabs (Sheet1, Sheet2 etc.) to move between workbooks

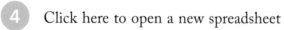

Adding data and calculating a total

To add data to a spreadsheet and calculate a total:

1 Click in a cell and add either text or numbers

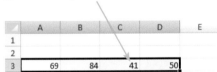

2 Press Enter or click here to confirm the data entry

3 To perform a calculation on a row or column, highlight the required items

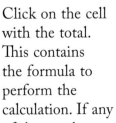

4 Click here to add the selected items

5 The result is shown in the cell next to the selected items

6 Click on the cell with the total. This contains the formula to perform the calculation. If any of the numbers are edited, the formula will recalculate the total

Don't forget

It takes some time to become confident using Excel. For a comprehensive look at the program see "Excel 2007 in Easy Steps" in this series.

Hot tip

When a formula is used in a cell this is visible in the formula bar, underneath the toolbar at the top of the spreadsheet. Even though the cell itself will display a numerical value, the content of the cell is the formula.

Viewing photos

Digital photos are well established as part of everyday life and using them with a laptop is an excellent option: photos can be downloaded while you are away from home or traveling and they can easily be shown to other people via the mobile nature of a laptop. To view digital photos:

1 Click on the Start button, and click on the Pictures button on the Start Menu

2 Select a folder containing photos. Double-click on it to view the photos inside

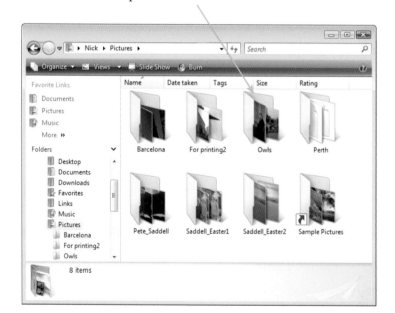

3 Click on this button to view the photos as a slide show

4 Select a photo and click on this button to open the photos in the selected folder in Windows Photo Gallery

5 The photos are displayed in the Windows Photo Gallery, with the selected one first

6 The controls at the bottom can be used to navigate around the photos. From left to right, they let you:

- Change the display size (zoom in or out)

- View the image at actual size

- Move to the previous photo

- View the photos in the folder as a slide show

- Move to the next photo

- Rotate the photo anticlockwise

- Rotate the photo clockwise

- Delete the photo

Don't forget

The toolbar at the top of the Windows Photo Gallery window has options for editing photos (see next page), finding out information about each photo, printing photos, emailing photos, burning (copying) photos to a CD or DVD or making them into a movie.

Editing photos

Digital photographs are seldom perfect the first time round and most of them benefit from some form of editing. This can be done within the Windows Photo Gallery. To do this:

78

1 Open a photo in the Windows Photo Gallery as shown on the previous two pages

2 Click on this button to access the editing tools

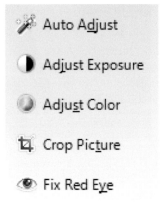

3 Use these buttons to perform the required editing tasks

4 The edited picture is displayed in the Windows Photo Gallery

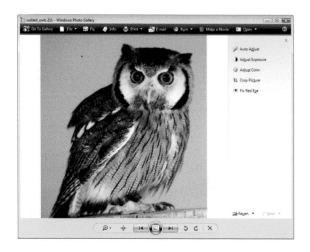

Downloading music

Digital music has enjoyed immense popularity in recent years, partly because of the number of sites that offer digital music for downloading and partly because of MP3 music players such as the iconic iPod from Apple.

Digital music can be downloaded from several online sites, and once this has been done it can be played on your laptop, copied onto an MP3 player and burned (copied) onto a CD or DVD. By default, when music is downloaded, it is placed in a sub-folder in the Music folder on your laptop.

The most popular online site for downloading music is Apple's iTunes, partly because of its association with the iPod. It is fairly representative of other commercial music downloading sites.

When downloading music the process is similar for all sites:

- Initially, you have to register on the site. This usually involves nothing more than a username, a password and credit card details for paying for the music you download

- You browse the site for the music in which you are interested

- Select the required music and select the "buy" function

- The music is downloaded into your Music folder

Managing music

Once music has been downloaded it can then be managed and listened to on your laptop. To do this:

1 Open the Windows Media Player as shown on page 72

2 Click here to view the categories within the Media Player

3 Initially the Media Player's Library will only contain preloaded content

Music can also be added to the Media Player by copying it from existing CDs (known as ripping). To do this, insert a music CD and select Rip from the Media Player menu bar. This will give you various options for copying the music from the CD.

4 To add content to the Media Player's Library, click on the Library button and select Add to Library

5 Select "My personal folders" to add content from your laptop

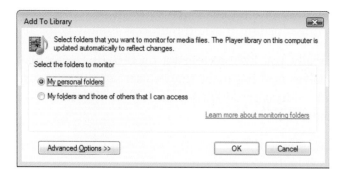

6 The appropriate content is accessed and placed in the relevant section of the Media Player

80

Listening to music

Once music has been added to the Media Player Library it can be listened to. To do this:

1 Click on Music Library and select a category

2 Select a song

3 Click on the play button

Creating a playlist

It is also possible to create playlists of your favorite music. To do this:

1 Click on Create Playlist and enter a name for the new playlist

2 Select a song or album and drag it into the newly created playlist

3 Click on the playlist name to view its contents

Hot tip

The Media Player can also be used to copy music onto CDs. To do this, insert a blank CD into your laptop's CD/DVD writer. Then select the items you want to burn (this can be done with songs, albums or playlists) and select Burn>Audio CD from the Media Player menu bar.

Downloading home movies

Through the use of digital video cameras it is now possible to download and view movies of family and friends on a laptop. To do this:

1. Connect the digital video camera to the laptop using a FireWire connection

2. Turn on the digital video camera and set it to playback

3. Open the Windows Movie Maker from the Start menu

 Windows Movie Maker

4. In the "Import" section, click on the "From digital video camera" link

Import ————————
From digital video camera
Videos
Pictures
Audio or Music

5. The Edit section can be used to access tools for editing your video footage

Edit ————————
Imported media
Effects
Transitions
Titles and credits

6. Once the video has been edited, it can be published to a variety of locations using the options in the "Publish to" section

Publish to ————————
This computer
DVD
Recordable CD
E-mail
Digital video camera

5 Internet and email

This chapter shows how to use your laptop on the Internet and how to perform popular tasks such as booking a holiday or sending an email.

Connecting to the Internet

The Internet is now a ubiquitous part of our lives. We use it for everything from viewing the news, to shopping, to online genealogy. With a laptop the possibilities for accessing the Internet are expanded to almost any location, not just when you are at home.

However, for all users it is first necessary to set up a home Internet connection. This is done by signing up with an internet service provider (ISP) who, for a fee, will provide you with a connection to the Internet.

Most ISPs provide high-speed DSL, broadband or cable access to the Internet, and for this you will need:

- A telephone line

- A router, which is the device that directs the Internet signal from your telephone line to your laptop

- A wireless or Ethernet connection for your laptop

If you have a wireless networking card in your laptop you will be able to connect to the router without the need for wires. Otherwise you will need to connect your router and your laptop with an Ethernet cable:

When you subscribe to an ISP they will provide you with any software that you need to connect to their service for the Internet (usually on a CD) and also any connection details that may be required, such as a username and a password. If these are required, you will only have to enter them once. After that your Internet connection should always be available when you turn on your laptop.

Don't forget

For a comprehensive guide to using the Internet, see "Internet for Seniors in Easy Steps" in this series.

Don't forget

There are hundreds of ISPs. Type "ISP" into Google to find an extensive list.

Making the connection

Once you have found an ISP and have the required
hardware in place you can then start connecting to the
Internet. In some cases this will involve following the
instructions provided by your ISP. However, it is also
possible to connect to the Internet using the Welcome
Center. To do this:

1 Access the Welcome Center as shown on page 64 of
Chapter 4

2 Click on this button

 Connect to the Internet

3 Click on the Connect to the
Internet link

4 Select an option for how you want to connect to the
Internet and follow the steps in the Wizard

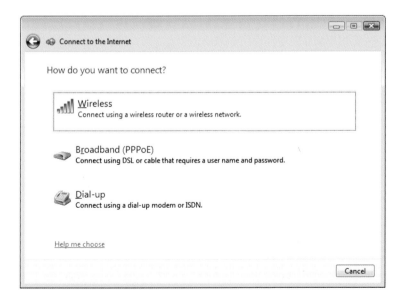

> **Don't forget**
>
> For more details
> about connecting to
> the Internet with a
> wireless connection,
> see Chapter 9.

85

Downloading new browsers

Browsers are the programs that allow people to navigate around the World-Wide Web (WWW) and view pages. They do this by interpreting the code that is used to create web pages and then displaying them in the graphical format to which we are now accustomed.

Windows Vista comes with the Internet Explorer browser pre-installed, but there are several other browsers that can be used to view the Web. These include Mozilla Firefox, Opera and Netscape Navigator. Of these, Firefox has been increasing in popularity. It is possible to download this browser to view the Web. To do this:

Don't forget

Opera can be downloaded at www.opera.com and Netscape Navigator can be downloaded at http://browser.netscape.com/ns8/

Beware

All new browsers should be free to download. If you are asked for a fee, cancel the process and look for another browser.

1 Go to the Firefox download page at www.mozilla.com

2 Click on this button to begin the downloading process

3 Once the download is complete the Firefox browser can be opened by clicking on this icon

Around the Web

When you are surfing the Web it is important to feel comfortable with both your browser and the websites at which you are looking. Most websites are a collection of linked pages that you can move between by clicking on links (also known as hyperlinks) that connect the different pages.

Address bar

The address bar is the box at the top of the browser that displays the address of the web page that is currently being viewed. Each web page has a unique address, so the address changes whenever you move to a different page. The address bar displays the web page address in this format:

Don't forget

The address for a website can be entered manually into the address bar or it can be selected from a list of favorites (see page 89).

Main content

The full content of a web page is displayed in the main browser window:

...cont'd

Hot tip

The toolbar contains a "home page" button which takes you to your own home page, i.e. the page that is accessed when you first open up your browser. In Internet Explorer, the home page can be changed by selecting Tools and Internet Options from the menu bar and, under the General tab, entering the web address for your desired home page.

Don't forget

The items that make up the navigation bar are buttons, or textual links, that take you to another location within the site, or another website.

Toolbar

This is a collection of icons at the top of the browser that has various options for navigating around web pages, accessing options such as news feeds and printing pages:

Menu bar

This contains various menus with options for navigating around and customizing web pages. It is usually situated beneath the address bar:

Navigation bars

These are groups of buttons that appear on websites to help users navigate within the site. Generally, the main navigation bars appear in the same place on every page of the site:

Search box

Many websites have a search box, into which you can enter keywords or phrases to search over the whole site:

Links

These are the devices that are used to move between pages within a website, or from one website to another. Links can be in a variety of styles, but most frequently they are in the form of buttons, underlined text or a roll-over (i.e. a button or piece of text that changes appearance when the cursor is passed over it):

Tabs

Most current browsers have an option for using different tabs. This enables you to open different web pages within the same browser window. You can then move between the pages by clicking on the tabs, at the top of the window:

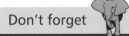

Favorites

Everyone has their favorite web pages that they return to again and again. These can be added to a list in a browser so that they can be accessed quickly when required. There is usually a button at the top of the browser that can add the current page to the list of favorites:

Don't forget

The cursor usually turns into a pointing hand when is it over a link on a website.

Don't forget

In some browsers, favorites are known as bookmarks, but they are the same thing.

Don't forget

A list of favorites, or bookmarks, can be accessed by clicking on the "favorites", or "bookmarks", link on the browser's menu bar. This can also be used to add a page to the favorites list.

89

Shopping on your laptop

Some people love physically going around shops, while for others it is a chore. For the latter group, online shopping is one of the great innovations of the Web, and even for the former group it can be invaluable when there is not the time or opportunity to go to actual shops. With a laptop, it is possible to do your shopping in the comfort of your own home while avoiding the crowds.

When you are shopping online there are some guidelines that you should follow to try and ensure you are in a safe online environment and do not spend too much money:

● Make a note of what you want to buy and stick to this once you have found it. Online shopping sites are adept at displaying a lot of enticing offers and it is a lot easier to buy something by clicking a button than it is to physically take it to a checkout

● Never buy anything that is promoted to you via an email, unless it is from a company whom you have asked to send you promotional information

● When paying for items, make sure that the online site has a secure area for accepting payment and credit-card details. A lot of sites display information about this within their payment area, and another way to ascertain this to check in the address bar of the payment page. If it is within a secure area the address of the page will start with "https" rather than the standard "http"

Don't forget

A lot of online shopping sites list recommendations for you based on what you have already looked at or bought on the site. This is done by using "cookies", which are small programs that are downloaded from the site and then track the items that you look at on the site.

https://www.amazon

Using online shopping

The majority of online shopping sites are similar in their operation:

- Goods are identified

- Goods are placed in a shopping basket

- Once the shopping is completed you proceed to the checkout

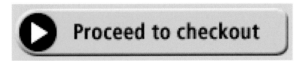

- You enter your shipping details and pay for the goods, usually with a credit card

On some sites you have to register before you can buy goods and in some cases this enables you to perform your shopping more quickly by using a one-click system. This means that all of your billing and payment details are already stored on the site and you can buy goods simply by clicking one button without having to re-enter your details. One of the most prominent sites to use this method is Amazon:

Beware

One-click shopping is an effective way to spend money very quickly. However, you usually have a period of time in which you can cancel your purchases after you have bought them in this way.

Booking a vacation

Just as a lot of retailers have created an online presence, the same is also true for vacation companies and travel agents. It is now possible to book almost any type of vacation on the Web, from cruises to city breaks.

Several sites offer full travel services where they can deal with flights, hotels, insurance, car hire and excursions. These sites include:

- Expedia at www.expedia.com
- Travelocity at www.travelocity.com
- Tripadvisor at www.tripadvisor.com

These sites usually list special offers and last-minute deals on their home pages and there is also a facility for specifying your precise requirements. To do this:

1 Select your vacation requirements

2 Enter flight details (if applicable)

3 Enter dates for your vacation

4 Click on the Search button

In addition to sites that do everything for you it is also possible to book your vacation on individual sites. This can be particularly useful for cruises and also for booking hotels around the world. Some websites to look at are:

Cruises

- Cruises.com at www.cruises.com

- Carnival at www.carnival.com

- Princess Cruises at www.princess.com

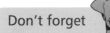

Don't forget

Vacation and hotel websites usually have versions that are specific to your geographical location.

Hotels

- Hotels.com at www.hotels.com

- All-hotels at www.all-hotels.com

- Choice Hotels International at www.choicehotels.com

Researching family history

A recent growth industry on the Web has been family history, or genealogy. Hundreds of organizations around the world have now digitized their records concerning individuals and family histories, and there are numerous websites that provide online access to these records. Some of these sites are:

● Ancestry at www.ancestry.com

● Genealogy.com at www.genealogy.com

● Familysearch at www.familysearch.org

● RootsWeb.com at www.rootsweb.com

Most genealogy sites require you to register, for a fee, before you can conduct extensive family research on their sites, but once you have done the process is similar on them all:

94

 Enter the details of the family members in the search boxes

 Click on the search button

Search For Your Ancestors
Enter all known information about deceased ancestor.

Albert	Vandome
First Name	Last Name

All	▾	1900	+ or - 20 year ▾
Life Event		Year	Year Range

All Countries	▾		▾
Country			

Search   Advanced Search

3 The results are displayed for the names searched against

Results for: Albert Vandome
Any Event, 1880 - 1920, All Countries
Exact Spelling: Off
Matches: All Sources - 1
Census - 1881 British Census
1. Albert D. VANDAM - 1881 British Census / Middlesex
Head   Gender: Male   Birth: <1853> Amsterdam (F), The Netherlands
Matches: Census/1881 British Census - 1

Using email

As a means of communication email has a great many benefits: it is fast, it is cheap and it can contain large amounts of information in the form of attachments.

If you have an Internet account with an ISP this should include an email account and you should receive an email address when you subscribe to your ISP. Once you have this you will be able to send and receive email using any email program. The most common ones for Windows users are Outlook and Outlook Express, and Windows Mail is common for Vista users.

Account details

Once you have an email account created you will be able to view the account details within your email program. To do this (for Windows Mail):

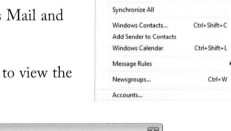

1   Open Windows Mail and select Tools

2   Click Accounts to view the account details:

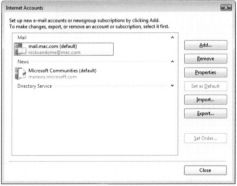

95

Don't forget

By default, messages should be downloaded to your email program every few minutes, but if you want to see if you have any messages as quickly as possible, the Send/ Receive button can be used for this purpose.

Receiving emails

Once your account is active you can check to see if you have any messages by clicking on the Send/Receive button.

...cont'd

Emailing family and friends
To compose a new email (using Windows Mail):

1 Click on the Create Mail button

2 Enter the email address of the recipient here

3 Enter the subject for the email here

4 Enter the text for the email here

5 Use these buttons to format the text

6 Click on the Send button

Including attachments
Attachments are a popular way to include photographs and documents with an email. To do this:

Beware

Emails with large attachments (over 1 Mb) take longer to send and download.

1 Click on this button

2 Select a file from your hard drive

3 The file is added to the email in the Attach box

Subject: Photos of grandchildren

Attach: barcelona02.jpg (35.6 KB)

6 Sharing with your family

This chapter shows how different people can securely share your laptop.

About multiple users

Because of the power and flexibility that is available in a laptop computer, it seems a waste to restrict it to a single user. Thankfully, it is possible for multiple users to use the same laptop. One way to do this is simply to let different people use the laptop whenever they have access to it. However, since everyone creates their own files and documents, and different people use different types of programs, it makes much more sense to allow people to set up their own user accounts. This creates their own personal computing area that is protected from anyone else accessing it. User accounts create a sense of personalization, and also security as each account can be protected by a password.

Without user accounts, the laptop will automatically display the desktop when it is turned on. However, if different user accounts have been set up on the laptop, a list of these accounts will be displayed when the computer is turned on:

Nick
Administrator
Password protected

Eilidh
Standard user

Peter
Standard user

Guest
Guest account

The relevant user can then click on their own account to access it. At this point they may have to enter their password to gain access to their own account. A password can be added to every user account, but there is no requirement to do so. However, if an account does not have a password, anyone can access that user's account, as long as they have access to the laptop. It is good practice to add a password for every user who has a separate account on the laptop. To see how to set user passwords see pages 100–101.

Hot tip

A Guest user account is available by default and this can be used by anyone. If multiple accounts have been set up this appears as one of the options.

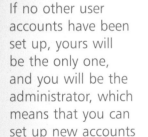

Don't forget

If no other user accounts have been set up, yours will be the only one, and you will be the administrator, which means that you can set up new accounts and alter a variety of settings on the laptop.

Customization

Once individual accounts have been set up, it is possible for each individual user to customize their account, i.e. to set the way in which their account appears and operates. This means that each user can set their own preferences, such as desktop background image, icon size and screensaver:

Don't forget

By default, all software on the laptop is available to all users. See page 108 to see how you can restrict access to certain programs, if required.

Managing your own account

If you are going to be using multiple user accounts, i.e. more than one, then you will need to specify some settings for your own account. By default, you are the administrator of the computer, which means that you have the access permissions to set up accounts and edit their settings. This also means that, before any other accounts are added, the laptop will open automatically with your desktop showing. However, once new accounts are created, each one could require a password, so you should also add a password to your own account. To do this:

Don't forget

Your account name is the one that you enter when you first start using your laptop. This can be changed in the User Accounts section, if required.

Beware

If you do not protect your own user account with a password, anyone with access to your laptop will be able to view your personal files and information.

1 Click on the Start button

2 Click on the Control Panel button

3 Click on the User Accounts and Family Safety link

User Accounts and Family Safety
Set up parental controls for any user
Add or remove user accounts

4 Under User Accounts, click on the "Change your Windows password" link

User Accounts
Change your account picture
Change your Windows password

5 Your account information is displayed here

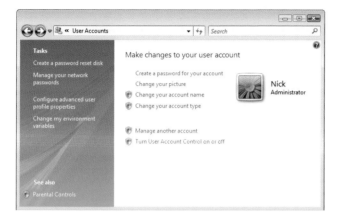

Hot tip

When creating or changing a password there is also an option for changing the image that is used to illustrate your account. This can be changed to one of the library images, or you can select one of your own photographs from your hard drive.

6 Click on "Create a password for your account"

101

7 Enter your password and enter it again to confirm it

8 Enter a hint to remind you of your password if you forget it and click on the "Create password" button

Don't forget

Once you have set a password for yourself you will have to enter it every time you turn on your laptop.

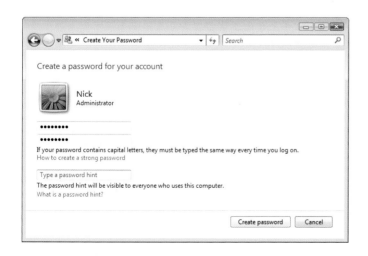

Adding family users

You can add new user accounts, such as for other family members, in a similar way to editing information about your own account. To do this:

 Click on the Start button

 Click on the Control Panel button

 Click on the User Accounts and Family Safety link

User Accounts and Family Safety
Set up parental controls for any user
Add or remove user accounts

 Click on the "Add or remove user accounts" link

User Accounts
Change your account picture | Add or remove user accounts
Change your Windows password

 The existing accounts are displayed in the Manage Accounts window

6 Click on the "Create a new account" link

Create a new account

7 Enter a name for the new account

Name the account and choose an account type

This name will appear on the Welcome screen and on the Start menu.

Peter

◉ Standard user

8 Check on the "Standard user" button

9 The new user is added to the Manage Accounts window

10 Click on a user account to view its details. A password can be created for the new account in the same way as adding a password for your own account as shown on pages 100–101

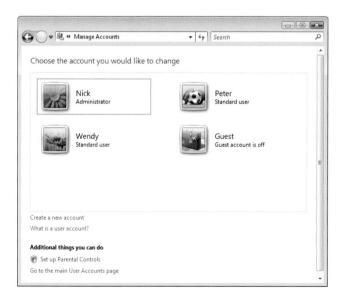

Beware

It is possible to change the type of an account so that anyone can be an administrator (in the User Accounts section). However, this would give them complete access to the laptop, and other user accounts, and enable them to make system changes that affect other users.

Parental Controls

Once multiple user accounts have been set up it is possible to apply separate security settings to different accounts. This can be particularly useful if you are going to be setting up an account for grandchildren and you want to have a certain amount of control over how they use the laptop. To do this:

1 Access the Users Accounts and Family Safety section of the Control Panel as shown on page 100

2 Click on Parental Controls

3 Click on a user for whom you want to set parental controls

4 The User Controls window contains options for specifying settings for how the user is allowed to use the computer

5 Check on this button to turn on Parental Controls

Parental Controls:

◉ On, enforce current settings

Web controls

One of the most common uses of computers for young people is the Web, but it is not always possible to monitor what they are using it for all of the time. In order to try and control this, the Web controls can be used in the Parental Controls section. To do this:

1 Click on this link to specify how the user can operate on the Web

 Windows Vista Web Filter
Control allowed websites, downloads, and other use

2 Check on the "Block some websites or content" button to be able to block certain types of content

Which parts of the Internet can Eilidh visit?

⦿ Block some websites or content

○ Allow all websites and content

3 Enter a website address here

Website address:

http://www.badgames.com

4 Click on one of these buttons to allow or block the site

Allow   Block

5 Check this button if you only want the user to be able to access the sites on the allow list

☑ Only Allow websites which are on the allow list

105

...cont'd

6 Click on the OK button

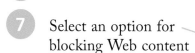

OK

7 Select an option for blocking Web content

Block web content automatically

Choose a web restriction level:

● High ○ Medium

8 Check this button if you want to stop any files from being downloaded from the Web by this user

☑ Block file downloads

9 Click on the OK button

OK

Time controls

A familiar worry when young people are using computers is the amount of time that they are spending on them. However, this can also be controlled in the Parental Controls section. To do this:

1 Click on this link to specify times at which a user can use the computer

Time limits
Control when Eilidh uses the computer

2 Click on the squares for times at which you do not want the specified user to use the computer. The blocked times are colored blue

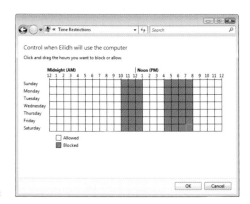

3 Click on the OK button

OK

Games controls

Computer games are another very popular pastime for young people. These include games that are downloaded from the Web and also those that are bought on CDs or DVDs. However, just as with movies, some games are unsuitable for younger children and should have ratings to specify the age groups for which they are suitable. It is then possible to control which games are played. To do this:

1 Click on the Games link to specify the games that a user can use on the computer

Games
Control games by rating, content, or title

2 Check on the Yes button to allow the user to play games

Can Eilidh play games?

⦿ Yes

◯ No

3 Click on the "Set game ratings" link to specify the ratings level of the games that the user can play

Block (or allow) games by rating and content types

Set game ratings

4 Check on a button to specify a ratings level

EARLY CHILDHOOD
Titles rated EC - Early Childhood have content that may be suitable for ages 3 and older.
Titles in this category contain no material that parents would find inappropriate.

5 Click on the OK button

OK

...cont'd

6 Click on this link to block or allow specific games

Block (or allow) any game on your computer by name

Block or Allow specific games

7 Click on these buttons to specify how games are accessed

Title/Rating	Status	User Rating Setting	Always Allow	Always Block
Chess Titans E	Can play	○	◉	○

8 Click on the OK button   [OK]

 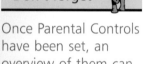
Program controls

It is possible to control which programs on your laptop a certain person can use. To do this:

1 Click on this link to specify the programs that a user can use on the computer

Allow and block specific programs
Allow and block any programs on your computer

2 Check on this button to specify programs the user can access

Which programs can Eilidh use?
○ Eilidh can use all programs
◉ Eilidh can only use the programs I allow

3 Check on a button to allow the user to access a program

Check the programs that can be used:

File	Description
☑ 🎬 MOVIEMK.exe	Windows Movie Maker
☑ 🎥 VideoCameraAutoPlay...	Windows Video Camera Auto Pla...

4 Click on the OK button   [OK]

7 On vacation

Laptops are ideal for taking on vacation and this is now a realistic proposition for anyone. This chapter looks at the issues of taking your laptop with you and keeping it safe. It also shows how to perform various vacation tasks.

Transporting your laptop

When you are going on vacation your laptop can be a very valuable companion. It can be used to download vacation photographs from a digital camera, download home movies from a digital video camera, keep a diary of your vacation, and keep a record of your itinerary and important documents, and in many parts of the world it can access the Internet via wireless hotspots so that you can view the Web and send emails. However, when you are traveling with your laptop it is sensible to transport this valuable asset in as safe and secure a way as possible. Some of the options include:

Laptop case
A standard laptop case is a good option for when you are on vacation: it is compact, lightweight and designed to accommodate your laptop and its accessories.

Metal case
If you are concerned that your laptop may be in danger of physical damage on your vacation you may want to consider a more robust metal case. These are similar to those used by photographers and, depending on its size and design, you may also be able to include your photographic equipment.

Backpacks
A serious option for transporting your laptop on vacation is a small backpack. This can either be a standard backpack or a backpack specifically designed for a laptop. The latter is clearly a better option as the laptop will fit more securely and there are also pockets designed for accessories:

Don't forget

A backpack for carrying a laptop can be more comfortable than a shoulder bag as it distributes the weight more evenly.

Keeping your laptop safe

By most measures, laptops are valuable items. However, in a lot of countries around the world their relative value can be a lot more than it is to their owners: in some countries the value of a laptop could easily equate to a month's, or even a year's, wages. Even in countries where their relative value is not so high they can still be seen as a lucrative opportunity for thieves. Therefore it is important to try and keep your laptop as safe as possible when you are on vacation. Some points to consider in relation to this are:

- If possible, try and keep your laptop with you at all times, i.e. transport it in a piece of luggage that you can carry rather than having to put it into a large case

- Never hand over your laptop, or any other of your belongings, to any local who promises to look after them

- If you do have to detach yourself from your laptop, try and put it somewhere secure such as a hotel safe

- When you are traveling, try and keep your laptop as unobtrusive as possible. This is where a backpack carrying case can prove useful as it is not immediately apparent that you are carrying a laptop

- Do not use your laptop in areas where you think it may attract undue interest from the locals, particularly in obviously poor areas. For instance, if you are in a local cafe the appearance of a laptop may create unwanted attention for you. If in doubt, wait until you get back to your hotel

- If you are accosted by criminals who demand your laptop then hand it over. No piece of equipment is worth suffering physical injury for

- Make sure your laptop is covered by your vacation insurance. If not, get separate insurance for it

- Trust your instincts with your laptop. If something doesn't feel right then don't do it

Hot tip

Save your important documents, such as vacation photos, onto a pen drive or CD/DVD on a daily basis when on vacation and keep this away from your laptop. This way you will still have these items if your laptop is lost or stolen.

Temperature extremes

Traveling consists of seeing a lot of different places and cultures but it also invariably involves different extremes of temperature: a visit to the pyramids of Egypt can see the mercury in the upper reaches of the thermometer, while a cruise to Alaska would encounter much colder conditions. Whether it is hot or cold, looking after your laptop is an important consideration in extremes of temperature.

Heat

When travelling in hot countries the best way of avoiding damage to your laptop is to prevent it from getting too hot in the first place:

- Do not place your laptop in direct sunlight

- Keep your laptop insulated from the heat

- Do not leave your laptop in an enclosed space, such as a car. Not only can this get very hot, but the sun's power can be increased by the vehicle's glass

Cold

Again, it is best to try and avoid your laptop getting too cold in the first place and this can be done by following similar precautions as for heat. However, if your laptop does suffer from extremes of cold, allow it to warm up to normal room temperature again before you try to use it. This may take a couple of hours, but it will be worth the wait, rather than risking damaging the delicate computing elements inside.

Laptops at sea

Water is the greatest enemy of any electrical device, and laptops are no different. This is of particular relevance to anyone who is taking their laptop on vacation near water, such as on a cruise. This not only has the obvious element of water in the sea but also the proliferation of swimming pools that are included on cruise ships. If you are going on vacation near water then bear the following in mind:

- Avoid water. The best way to keep your laptop dry is to keep it away from water whenever possible. For instance, if you want to update your diary or download some photographs, then it would be best to do this in an indoor environment, rather than sitting around the pool

- Keeping dry. If you think you will be transporting your laptop near water then it is a good precaution to protect it with some form of waterproof bag. There are a range of "dry-bags" that are excellent for this type of occasion and they remain waterproof even if fully immersed in water. These can be bought from outdoor suppliers

- Drying out. If the worst does occur and your laptop does get a good soaking then all is not lost. However, you will have to ensure that it is fully dried out before you try and use it again

Power sockets

Different countries and regions around the world use different types of power sockets, and this is an issue when you are on vacation with your laptop. Wherever you are going in the world it is vital to have an adapter that will fit the sockets in the countries you intend to visit. Otherwise you will not be able to charge your laptop.

There are over a dozen different types of plugs and sockets used around the world, with the four most popular being:

North America, Japan
This is a two-point plug and socket. The pins on the plug are flat and parallel.

Continental Europe
This is a two-point plug and socket. The pins are rounded.

Australasia, China, Argentina
This is a three-point socket that can accommodate either a two- or a three-pin plug. In a two-pin plug, the pins are angled in a V shape.

UK
This is a three-point plug. The pins are rectangular.

114

Airport security

Because of the increased global security following terrorist attacks such as those of September 11 2001, the levels of airport security have been greatly increased around the world. This has implications for all travelers, and if you are traveling with a laptop this will add to the security scrutiny which you will face. When dealing with airport security when traveling with a laptop there are some issues that you should always keep in mind:

- Keep your laptop with you at all times. Unguarded baggage at airports immediately raises suspicion and it can make life very easy for thieves

- Carry your laptop in a small bag so that you can take it on board as hand luggage. On no account should it be put in with your luggage that goes in the hold

- X-ray machines at airports will not harm your laptop. However, if anyone tries to scan it with a metal detector, ask them if they can inspect it by hand instead

- Keep a careful eye on your laptop when it goes through the X-ray conveyor belt and try and be there at the other side as soon as it emerges. There have been some stories of people causing a commotion at the security gate just after someone has placed their laptop on the conveyor belt. While everyone's attention (including yours) is distracted, an accomplice takes the laptop from the conveyor belt. If you are worried about this you can ask for the security guard to hand-check your laptop rather than putting it on the conveyor belt

- Make sure the battery of your laptop is fully charged. This is because you may be asked to turn on your laptop to verify that it is just that, and not some other device disguised as a laptop

- When you are on the plane, keep the laptop in the storage area under your seat, rather than in the overhead locker, so that you know where it is at all times

Beware

If there is any kind of distraction when you are going through security checks at an airport it could be because someone is trying to divert your attention in order to steal your laptop.

115

Hot tip

When traveling through airport security, leave your laptop in Sleep mode so that it can be powered up quickly if anyone needs to check that it works properly.

Downloading photos

Vacations are a great time for taking digital photographs, and a laptop provides the means to download them from the camera. This enables you to view and edit photographs on your laptop and it also allows you to clear your camera's memory card while on vacation. You can then continue taking your vacation snaps. There are two main ways in which photos can be downloaded, using Windows Vista. These are with the Windows Import function or the Windows Photo Gallery

Using Windows Import
The Windows Import function enables digital photographs to be downloaded directly from a digital camera or a memory-card reader. To do this:

Don't forget

Tags can be used for searching for photographs once they have been downloaded.

1 Connect the digital camera or card reader to your laptop

2 In the AutoPlay window (which should open automatically), click on the "Import pictures using Windows" option

3 If desired, you can add tags to the images when they are downloaded

4 Click on the Import button   Import

5 The photos are downloaded automatically

6 Once the images have been downloaded they are displayed in the Windows Photo Gallery

Don't forget

When you download your photographs from your memory card you can clear the memory card to capture more photographs. However, make sure that you back up the items on your laptop by copying them onto a CD, a DVD or a pen drive.

117

...cont'd

Using Windows Photo Gallery

Windows Photo Gallery is a versatile program for downloading, organizing and editing digital photographs. To use it for downloading photographs:

1 Click on the Start button

2 Select the Windows Photo Gallery button from the Start Menu, or click on the All Programs link and select it from here

3 In the Windows Photo Gallery select File>Import from Camera or Scanner from the Menu bar

4 Select the device from which you want to download your photographs

5 Click on the Import button

6 The Importing Pictures and Videos window opens and photographs can be downloaded in the same way as described on the previous two pages

Hot tip

Photographs can also be added to the Windows Photo Gallery from any location on your laptop. To do this, select File>Add Folder to Gallery from the Menu bar. Then navigate to the folder you want to include.

Organizing photos

When on vacation it is human nature to take as many photographs as possible, and with digital cameras it is easy to capture hundreds of photos since you are not using up any film. This is not a problem but it can mean that you quickly find you have several hundred vacation photographs on your laptop. When you first download them you will probably remember everything about them. However, once you return home you may forget some of the finer details of the photographs and, as your collection grows and grows, this could result in it becoming harder to find the photographs that you want. This problem can be overcome by organizing them in the Windows Photo Gallery.

Accessing photos

To access and view specific photos:

1. Click on a specific date, in the left-hand pane, to view images that were taken on that date

2. The images that match the selected date are displayed in the Windows Photo Gallery window

Beware

Make sure that you set the time and date on your digital camera before you first start to use it. Otherwise, the time and date will be incorrect as far as the Windows Photo Gallery is concerned.

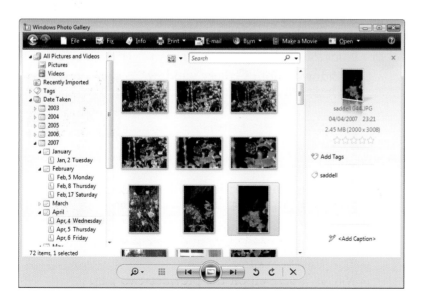

...cont'd

Tagging photos

An excellent way to make photographs easier to find is to give them tags. These are keywords, or phrases, that help identify the photograph in terms of time, place, location or subject matter. To do this:

1 Click here to create a new tag

◢ 🗩 Tags
　　🗩 *Create a New Tag*

2 Type the name for the new tag

◢ 🗩 **Tags**
　　💗 **Flowers**

3 Select a photograph in the Windows Photo Gallery window

4 Drag the photograph onto the tag name and release it; or

🗩 Recently Imported
◢ 🗩 Tags
　　🗩 Create a New Tag
　　🗩 Not Tagged
　　🗩 Flowers
◢ 🗩 Date Taken
　　▷ 🗩 2003

1 Click on a photograph in the Windows Photo Gallery window

2 The photograph and its details are displayed in the right-hand pane of the Windows Photo Gallery

saddell 051.JPG
04/04/2007　23:30
2.26 MB (3008 x 2000)
☆☆☆☆☆

🗩 Add Tags

3 Click on the Add Tags link   Add Tags

4 Enter a new tag name for the photograph ("Flowers")

 Add Tags

Flowers

Once tags have been added to photographs they can then be used to view all of the items with the same tag. To do this:

1 Click on a tag name

Tags
Create a New Tag
Not Tagged
Flowers

2 The matching photographs are displayed in the Windows Photo Gallery window

Flowers - 2 items

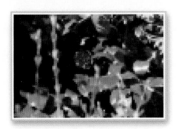 

121

...cont'd

Ranking photos

The nature of digital cameras ensures that it is very easy to take a lot of similar photographs of the same subjects, to make sure you get a good one. Once they have been downloaded it is possible to use Windows Photo Gallery to rank them so that you can quickly view the photographs that you rate most highly. To do this:

122

1 Click on a photograph in the Windows Photo Gallery window

2 The selected photograph is displayed in the right-hand pane of the Windows Photo Gallery

saddell_owls 229.JPG
04/04/2007   04:31
2.57 MB (2000 x 3008)

3 Click here to assign the required number of stars for the selected image

4 In the left-hand pane, click on a ratings level to view all of the items with that rating

Ratings

Sending photos

Before digital photographs became a ubiquitous part of our lives, it could be several weeks before vacation photographs were available for viewing. However, in the digital age, they can be sent to family and friends, via email, almost as soon as they have been taken. To do this:

1 Select a photograph in the Windows Photo Gallery window

Don't forget

The smaller the size of a photograph, the more quickly it will be emailed and received.

2 Click on the E-mail button on the Windows Photo Gallery menu bar

3 Click here to select the size at which you want the photograph to be sent

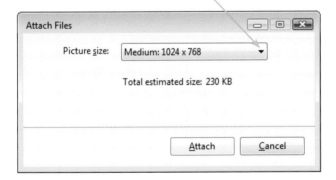

4 Click on the Attach button

5 Enter details of the email recipient and a message and click on the Send button

6 The photograph is attached to the email message

Keeping a diary

While on vacation, a diary is an excellent way to record your experiences and thoughts: what you might think is commonplace at the time can appear much more significant when you look back at it in months, or years, to come. As shown in Chapter 4, WordPad can be used for basic word processing, but for more flexibility and functionality, Microsoft Word is an excellent option for creating a comprehensive and attractive diary. To do this:

1 Click on the Start button and select  Microsoft Office Word 2007 from the Start Menu or from the All Programs button

2 The Word interface has tabs along the top to support various formatting functions

3 Select a font for the heading of your diary; or

4 Select a style for the heading

5 Enter the required heading

6 Do the same for any sub-headings you want to use and the body text of your diary

Making telephone calls

Just because you are on vacation does not mean that you cannot keep in touch with family and friends at home, and telephone calls via your laptop are an ideal way to do this. As long as you have access to the Internet you can make telephone calls around the world, using a program called Skype. Once this has been downloaded, you can make free telephone calls to anyone else who has Skype on their computer, and cheap ones to landlines or cell phones.

Downloading Skype
To download Skype ready for use on your laptop:

Don't forget

Skype is free to download and works with all major computer operating systems, such as Windows, Mac OS X and Linux.

1 Access the Skype homepage at www. skype.com

2 Click on this button to start the downloading process

3 Click on this button to continue

Download now

4 In the File Download window, click on the Run button

5 The Download window displays the progress of the downloading process

...cont'd

6   In the User Account Control window, click on the Continue button

7   In the Install window, select the required language and check box 2 to accept the User License Agreement

8   Click on the Install button

9   Click on the Finish button

...cont'd

Adding contacts

Before you start making telephone calls with Skype you have to add the contacts whom you want to call. To do this:

1 Click on this icon to launch Skype, or select it from the All Programs menu on the Start Menu

 Skype

2 In the Skype window, click on the Contacts tab

 Contacts

3 To add details of another Skype user that you know, click on the Add Contact button

 Add Contact

4 Enter the Skype name of the person you want to contact and click on the Find button

5 Select the person you want to add as a contact and click on the Add Skype Contact button

6 Enter a message to be sent to the new contact

7 Click on the OK button

 OK

Don't forget

Before you start using Skype you can test your sound through the Skype Test Call option that is available in the Skype window.

Hot tip

You can also find other Skype users by clicking on the Search for Skype Users link. Here you can enter someone's name and see if they have a Skype account. If they do, you can then add them as a contact.

127

...cont'd

Making a call

To make a telephone call to another Skype user:

 In the Skype window, click on the Contacts tab

 Click on a contact name

 Click on the green telephone icon to make the call. The other user has to accept the call once it has been made to activate it. They do this by clicking on their Answer button

Click on the red telephone icon to end the call (this can be done by either user)

Click on the Call Phones tab to make a call by entering a specific telephone number

8 Laptop networking

Home networking has been one of the great advances in computing of recent years and it means that a laptop can be connected to other computers from anywhere in the home. This chapter shows how to set up and manage a home network and how to securely share information with other people.

What is a network?

In computing terms a network is two, or more, computers that are connected together to share data or share an Internet connection. This means that if two computers are connected to a network they can both use the same Internet connection and also swap any files between them without the need to copy them onto a form of removable storage such as a CD, DVD or pen drive.

The most basic form of a network is when two computers are connected together using a cable. This is usually done with what is called an Ethernet cable. The cable is connected to each computer and then the network can be created:

Each computer can then create a Public area in which files and folders can be stored. Any items in the Public area can then be accessed by any other computer connected to the network.

In order for the two computers to communicate with each other on the network, they need to have a network card, which enables each computer to link to the network and be seen by the other.

Don't forget

In addition to computers, networks can also have items such as printers connected to them. This means that each of the computers on the network can use the networked printer.

Hot tip

Most modern laptops come with network capabilities, i.e. a network card. To check this, access the Control Panel and click on the Hardware and Sound link. Under Device Manager, click on the "View hardware and devices" link. Double-click on Network Adapters to view the installed components.

Local-area network (LAN)

A more common form of network is one where the computers are connected via a hardware device, known as a router, which is usually also connected to the Internet. The router acts a hub for the network: all of the attached computers communicate via the router, which passes on the requested information to each computer on the network. For home users, this type of network is known as a local-area network (LAN) because it occupies a relatively small area, usually within the confines of the home.

A LAN can be created with cable connections and also with wireless connectivity. Most routers support both of these types of connection. The router is also usually the means by which the Internet is disseminated around the network: the Internet connection is passed through the router and then communicated to the attached computers.

So a simple LAN would consist of a router that is connected to two computers, either wirelessly or via Ethernet cables:

Don't forget

Computer networks can be vast, consisting of thousands of connected computers and covering different countries and continents. These are known as wide-area networks (WANs).

131

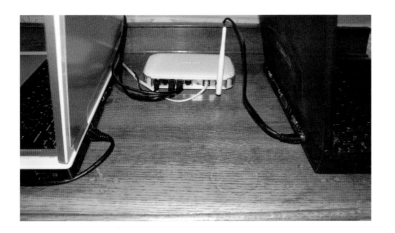

Don't forget

A local network that operates wirelessly is known as a wireless local-area network (WLAN).

Network and Sharing Center

When you are working with networks, one area with which you will become familiar is the Network and Sharing Center. This is used to show your network settings and operations and also to specify a variety of settings for how your networks operate and perform. To access the Network and Sharing Center:

1 Click on the Start button

2 Click on the Control Panel button

3 Click on the Network and Internet link

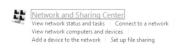

Network and Internet
View network status and tasks
Set up file sharing

4 Click on the Network and Sharing Center link

Network and Sharing Center
View network status and tasks   Connect to a network
View network computers and devices
Add a device to the network | Set up file sharing

5 The Network and Sharing Center contains all of the information you need to set up a network

6 In the Sharing and Discovery section, there are various options for managing a network

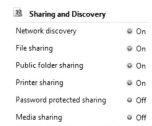

Joining two computers

The simplest form of a computer network is known as a peer-to-peer network, using an Ethernet cable. This is when two computers are connected together to share information with each other. This is ideal for laptop users as it enables them to set up a network with other laptop users and also with static desktop computers. This type of network does not have a connection to the Internet: it is just for sharing files on individual computers. To do this:

1 Connect two computers with an Ethernet cable as shown on page 130

2 The network connection is shown in the Network and Sharing Center (there is no Internet connection)

View full map

NICK-LAPTOP (This computer) — Unidentified network — ✖ — Internet

3 Click on the "View computers and devices" link to view the networked computers

View computers and devices

4 The networked computers are displayed in the Network window. Double-click on one to view its accessible folders and files

Hot tip

Click on the "View full map" link to see how the computers in the network are connected to each other (see page 138 for further details about this).

Beware

If you cannot access the contents of a computer that has been networked in this way, it could be because its firewall settings are blocking access. Check the firewall settings to see if it is preventing network access.

Hardware for a network

The next step up from a peer-to-peer network is one where multiple devices, e.g. several computers, printers and an Internet connection, can be joined together. You may want to set up a network for a variety of reasons, such as sharing your Internet connection between two, or more, computers, or copying files from a desktop computer onto your laptop. To do this you have to first get all of the required hardware in place. For this you will require a router, which is the device through which all of the elements of the network will communicate. To do this:

Beware

If your network uses a wireless router, this means that anyone within the range of the router could connect to the network, even if they are outside your house. To avoid this you have to set a password for your router, which can be done when you initially connect it.

1　Plug in your router to the mains electricity

2　Connect your router to your Internet connection, via either a phone line or a cable. This usually plugs into the back of the router

3　For a cable connection, attach one end of the cable into the computer and the other into the router

4   If you have a laptop with wireless connectivity, this does not need any additional connection: the laptop will communicate with the router wirelessly when the network software is accessed to create the network

Don't forget

For more information about setting up a wireless network, see Chapter 9.

5   Connect any other items of hardware that you want to include in the network, such as a printer. This can be done wirelessly, if the printer is equipped with a wireless card, or, more commonly, with a USB or an Ethernet connection

Beware

Not all routers have a USB connection, so you might not be able to connect a printer if this is its only form of connection. Instead, look for a printer with wireless connectivity.

Creating a cable network

Using Vista, when the hardware for a cable network is attached the network should be created automatically and be ready for use. The details of the network can be viewed in the Network and Sharing Center:

1 The elements of the network are displayed here

2 The type of network is displayed here. Since it is a cable network it is described as a "Local Area Connection", rather than a wireless one

Don't forget

A single computer connected to the Internet via a router still constitutes a network, as the router is considered part of the network.

NETGEAR (Private network)	
Access	Local and Internet
Connection	Local Area Connection

3 If any part of the network is not connected properly, the following graphic will be displayed

NICK-LAPTOP
(This computer)   Internet

Connecting more computers

Where networks really come into their own is when two or more computers are connected to the network. This enables the sharing of the Internet connection and also the sharing of files between computers. To add another computer to a network:

Hot tip

If you have grandchildren visiting, a shared Internet connection can be invaluable as it can help resolve arguments and disputes about Internet access.

1 Connect the Ethernet cable to the router and the computer in the same way as for connecting the first computer

2 The connection to the network is shown in the Network and Sharing Center

3 If the full network map is viewed this will display all of the computers connected to the network (for details on how to do this, see the following page)

Don't forget

The examples here and on the following pages are for connecting two computers running Windows Vista to a network. However, it is also possible to connect computers running Windows XP and this is looked at on pages 151–154.

137

Viewing a network

Once a network has been set up and computers have been connected to it, it is useful to be able to view all of the elements of the network. To do this:

1 In the Network and Sharing Center, each computer's connection is displayed

View full map

NICK-LAPTOP
(This computer)   NETGEAR   Internet

2 To see the whole network, click on the "View full map" link

View full map

3 All of the elements of the network are displayed

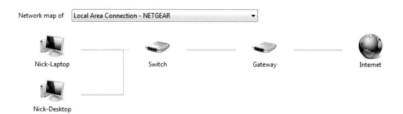

Network map of   Local Area Connection - NETGEAR

Nick-Laptop   Switch   Gateway   Internet

Nick-Desktop

Viewing computers

One of the purposes of a network is to enable you to share documents and files between different computers. For instance, you may have a lot of vacation photographs on your laptop that you want to share with a desktop computer, without having to email them or copy them onto a CD or DVD. Once the network has been set up it is possible to view the contents of the different computers on the network. To do this:

1 In the Network and Sharing Center, click on the Network icon; or

2 In the left-hand pane, click on the "View computers and devices" link

3 All of the computers and devices connected to the network are displayed

4 Double-click on a computer to view the available items within it

Don't forget

When you view a networked computer's contents, you will only be able to see the items that can be shared over the network. For more on this see page 145.

Sharing a network

Before sharing files between computers, the correct settings have to be applied so that each computer can give permission for other computers to view its files. For this to be done, settings have to be specified so that computers can initially see each other. Once this is done they have to then be given permission to share information. If the correct permissions are not set then the following window can appear when you try to access a computer on the network:

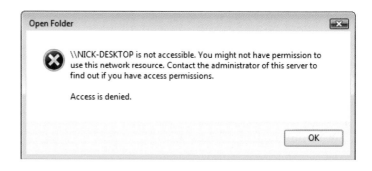

Don't forget

The Public setting can still be used for a network in the home, but it gives you more flexibility, and security, to set up a private one.

To set the correct permissions for file sharing:

1   In the Network and Sharing Center, the status of the networked computer (in this case "Public network") is displayed underneath the graphical representation

NICK-LAPTOP
(This computer)

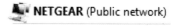

NETGEAR (Public network)

2   Click on the Customize link to change the status of the networked computer

3 Check on the Private button. This will enable all of the devices on your network to find this computer more easily and share all information with it. If you are using

a network within your own home then the Private option is the one that should be used

4 Click on the Next button

5 Check the settings and click on the Close button

141

6 Under the Sharing and Discovery section, click on the "Network discovery" button (by default it is off)

Sharing and Discovery

Network discovery   Off

7 Check on the "Turn on network discovery" button. This will enable this computer to find

    Turn on network discovery
    Turn off network discovery

other computers and devices on the network and communicate with them, and vice versa

...cont'd

8 If network discovery is turned off, a window like the following will appear when you try and view the other computers on the network (although they are still connected to the network, the computer cannot see them)

9 Once network discovery is turned on, all of the connected computers and devices are visible in the Network window (accessed by clicking on the "View computers and devices" link in the Network and Sharing Center window)

File sharing

Sharing files between computers is one of the fundamental uses for a network. Different users can view files from other computers and also edit and change them to create a collaborative working environment.

When a computer is connected to a network the majority of the files and programs on the computer are kept private from the network. This is a security measure to ensure that only the files that you want other people to see are available on the network. However, to enable sharing on the network, there is a Public folder into which documents and files can be copied. Other users on the network can then access the items from the Public folder. Each computer on the network has a Public folder, but it is possible to apply different settings for how it is accessed and used. To do this:

1 To view the available folders and files on a networked computer, access the Network window (as shown on the previous page)

2 Double-click on one of the computers on the network to view its contents

 NICK-DESKTOP

3 The available folders are displayed. These should include the Public folder

Beware

If you have a file open on one computer, you will not be able to share it on another, unless it is opened as read-only.

143

...cont'd

Specifying file sharing

In order for files to be shared between computers, they have to be told that this is allowable. To do this:

1 In the Network and Sharing Center window, the file-sharing options can be

viewed in the Sharing and Discovery section. Click on the "File sharing" button

2 Check on the "Turn on file sharing" button. This allows other users on the network to share files on your computer. Click on the Apply button

3 Click on the "Public folder sharing" button

Public folder sharing   ⊙ Off

4 Select one of the options

Saving files

When you want to save files so that other people on your network can access them, this can be done by either saving them into the Public folder on your own laptop, or saving them into the Public folder of another computer on your network. To do this:

1 Create the file that you want to save onto the network

2 First, save the file to a folder within your own file structure, i.e. one that is not visible on the network. This will ensure that you always have a master copy of the document

3 Select File>Save As from the menu bar (this is standard in most types of program)

4 The Save As window has options for where you can save the file

5 Click on the Network icon in the left-hand pane

Network

Don't forget

Files can also be copied to Public folders on the network by dragging and dropping them from within your own file structure. To access this, click on the Start button and click on the Computer button.

145

...cont'd

6 Double-click on your own computer if this is where you want to save the file; or

7 Double-click on another computer on the network to save the file here

8 Double-click on the Public folder icon

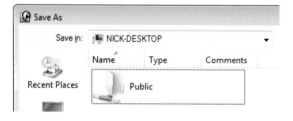

Beware

If you copy files to your own Public folder, other computers on the network will only be able to access these when your laptop is turned on.

9 Name the file that you want to save onto the network

File name: save1

10 Double-click on the folder into which you want to save the file

11 Click on the Save button

Sharing a printer

Once a network has been created it is then possible to connect other devices, so that they can be used by all of the computers connected to the network. The most common device to add in this way is a printer. In order to do this the printer has to be enabled for use on a network, i.e. it must be able to connect to a router through either a USB cable or an Ethernet one (or wirelessly). Once this is connected it is possible to share the printer on the network. To do this:

1 Access the Network and Sharing Center and click on the "View computers and devices" link

2 Click on the "Add a printer" button

3 In the Add Printer window, click on the "Add a network, wireless or Bluetooth printer" link (no need to click on the Next button)

4 In the Add Printer window, click any printers that are identified on the network

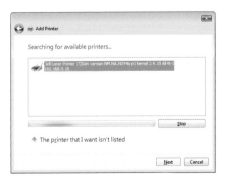

5 Click on the Next button

Hot tip

You should be able to find out if a printer is enabled for a network from its technical specification. More and more modern printers now come with this facility.

Don't forget

The printer must be connected to the router and turned on before it can be shared on a network.

147

...cont'd

6 Click on the printer name and click on the Next button to install the driver required for the printer

7 If the printer has been used as a stand-alone one, i.e. not a networked one, the driver will already have been installed. Click on the "Use the driver currently installed" button and click on the Next button

Don't forget

Each user on a network will have to add a networked printer individually to their own computer.

8 Give the printer a name and click on the Next button

9 Check on the "Share the printer so that others on your network can find and use it" button and click on the Next button

10 A confirmation window confirms that the printer has been installed. Click on the Finish button

Network security

Computer security is an important issue for all computer users and this is even more crucial when you allow other people access to your laptop and its files. In order to make your network as secure as possible, in addition to the normal virus and firewall protection, you can set a password so that only people with a user account and a password can view the Public folders on your laptop. You might want to do this if you are connected to a network that you have not set up, such as a wireless hotspot, where you do not want any of the other network users to be able to access your laptop. However, even when you have added password protection to your own laptop, you can still access all of the other elements of the network, unless they have been similarly protected. To add password protection for sharing your Public folder and its files:

Don't forget

For more information about general computer security see Chapter 10.

1   Open the Network and Sharing Center from the Control Panel (Network and Internet>Network and Sharing Center)

2   In the Sharing and Discovery section, click on the "Password protected sharing" button

...cont'd

3 Check on the "Turn on password protected sharing" button

◉ Turn on password protected sharing

◯ Turn off password protected sharing

—

4 Once password-protected sharing is turned on, anyone else on the network who tries to access your computer will see the following message:

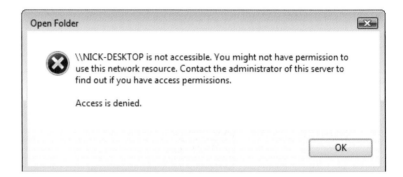

5 Even if your own laptop is protected on the network with a password, you can still access all of the other elements on the network

Networking with XP

If you are creating a network with other computers it may be the case that they are not all using the same operating system. For instance, one may be using Windows Vista while the other is still operating with Windows XP. To ensure that all of the computers on the network can communicate with each other, the network also has to be set up on the computer using Windows XP. To do this:

1. Click on the Start button

2. Click on the My Network Places button

Don't forget

The process for setting up a network with Windows XP is slightly longer than with Windows Vista, but it works just as effectively.

3. Click on the "Set up a home or small office network" link

4. In the Network Setup Wizard click on the Next button

5. The "Before you continue" window describes the items that are required for setting up a network. Click on the Next button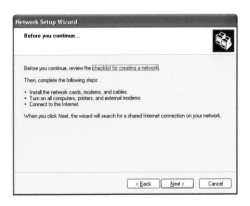

...cont'd

6 If you have already set up a network on another computer, click on the "Yes, use the existing shared connection for this computer's Internet access" button and click on the Next button

7 If you have more than one Internet connection, click on the "Determine the appropriate connections for me" button and then the Next button

8 Give the computer a description and a name and click on the Next button

9 Give your network a name by entering the name in the "Workgroup name" box. Click on the Next button

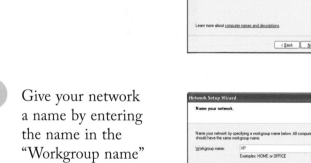

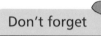

Don't forget

The computer name is the one that other users on the network will see when they are connected.

10 The network settings are displayed for review before they are applied. Click on the Next button

11 The following window is displayed while the network settings are applied

12 If you are using Vista on the other computer, click on the "Just finish the wizard, I don't need to run the wizard on other computers" button and click on the Next button

13 The following window is displayed to confirm the completion of the Network Setup Wizard. Click on the Finish button

...cont'd

14 If you check in My Network Places, you will see the items that are available on the network to which the Windows XP computer is connected

With a computer using Windows XP other users' Public folders can be accessed regardless of their computer's operating system, e.g. Vista or Mac OS X.

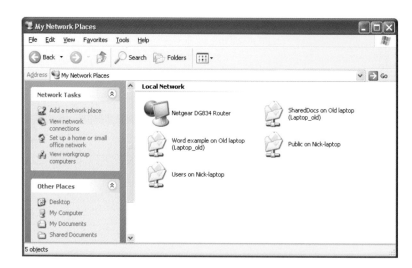

15 On the computer using Windows Vista the Network window includes the computer using Windows XP (in this instance LAPTOP_OLD)

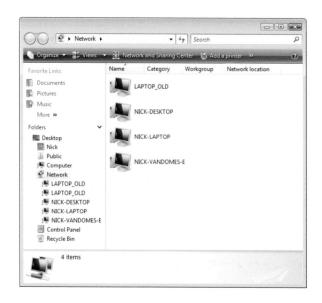

9 Going wireless

This chapter shows how you can get rid of a lot of cables around the home and connect to wireless networks in places such as airports and cafes.

Going wireless

In computing terms, "wireless" means connecting your computer to other devices using radio waves rather than cables. These can include a router for connecting to a network, a printer, keyboard, mouse or speakers (as long as these devices also have a wireless capability). For the laptop user in particular, this gives you the ultimate freedom: you can take your laptop wherever you want and still be able to access the Internet and use a variety of peripherals.

Wireless standards

As with everything in the world of computers, there are industry standards for wireless connections: for networking devices the standard is known as IEEE 802.11. The purpose of standards is to ensure that all of the connected devices can communicate with each other.

The IEEE 802.11 standard (or just 802.11) used for networks has a number of different variations (known as protocols) of the original standard. These variations have been developed since the introduction of 802.11 in 1997 with a view to making it work faster and cover a greater range. Early wireless devices used the 802.11a and 802.11b protocols, while the most widely used one at the time of writing is the 802.11g protocol. When you are creating a wireless network it is best to have all of the devices using the same version of 802.11. For instance, if you have a wireless card in your laptop that uses 802.11g then it is best to have the same version in your router. However, most modern wireless cards and routers have multiple compatibility and can cater for at least the b and g versions of the standard. If two devices are using different 802.11 protocols they should still be able to communicate with each other but the rate of data transfer will probably be slower than if both of the devices used the same protocol.

The Bluetooth standard is another method of connecting devices wirelessly. It does not have the same range as 802.11 and is generally now mainly used for connecting cellphones.

Don't forget

Very few new devices use the 802.11a version of the standard although newer devices will usually be backwards-compatible with it.

Don't forget

Devices using the 802.11g protocol can communicate with each other via radio waves over distances of approximately 25 yards (indoors) and 75 yards (outdoors).

Equipping your laptop

For a laptop to be able to connect wirelessly to a network, it needs to have a piece of hardware known as a wireless network adapter card. Most modern laptops have this pre-installed and details of it will be given in the laptop's specifications and literature. If a wireless network adapter card is fitted, this will be displayed in the Device Manager, which can be accessed via: Control Panel>System and Maintenance>System>Device Manager:

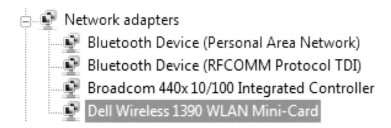

If your laptop does not have an internal wireless card, an external one can be inserted into one of the card slots at the side of the laptop. The card is inserted by pushing it into the slot until it clicks into place.

Hot tip

Instead of using a wireless card to equip your laptop for wireless networking, it is possible to attach a USB Network Adapter that performs the same purpose but is attached via the laptop's USB port.

Setting up a wireless router

In addition to having a wireless-enabled laptop, you will also require a wireless router in order for it to be able to communicate with your laptop and for you to set up a network. These are the same as cable routers except that they have a wireless card inside them (most of them also have Ethernet connections). Wireless routers are widely available at electrical and computer retailers and also at online retailers such as Amazon.

Once a wireless router has been plugged in and connected to a telephone line (for access to the Internet) it can then be configured so that it is ready for use. In some cases, this may happen automatically, but if it does not then you can do this through Vista (have the documentation that came with the router handy as this will contain information that you may be required to enter during the configuration process). To set up a wireless router for use on a network:

Hot tip

Look for a wireless router with both USB and Ethernet connections. This will give you greater flexibility in terms of attaching devices.

158

1. Access the Control Panel and click on the Network and Internet link

   Network and Internet
   View network status and tasks
   Set up file sharing

2. Click on the Network and Sharing Center link

   Network and Sharing Center
   View network status and tasks   Connect to a network
   View network computers and devices   Add a device to the network
   Set up file sharing

3. In the Network and Sharing Center, click on the "Set up a connection or network" link

   Set up a connection or network

4. Click on the "Set up a wireless router or access point" option

   Set up a wireless router or access point
   Set up a new wireless network for your home or small business

5. Click on the Next button   Next

6 In the next information window, click on the Next button

7 Vista then searches for information about the wireless router

8 In some cases Vista will not be able to configure the router automatically. If this is the case, click on this option

9 A page will open in your browser that is used to configure your router. This usually has an option for testing your wireless connection to make sure it is working

Hot tip

The router information page is where you can define security settings for your router. This involves selecting a type of security and then adding a password. This means that anyone else trying to connect to the network has to give the password to continue and connect to the router.

Connecting to the Internet

One of the simplest forms of network is a single computer connected to the Internet. Needless to say, this is a very important type of network and one that most people will use. Once the hardware for a wireless network has been set up (and the router is connecting to the Internet via a cable or a phone line) it is possible to connect wirelessly to the Internet. To do this:

1 In the Network and Sharing Center, click on the "Set up a connection or network" link

Set up a connection or network

2 Click on the "Connect to the Internet" option

Connect to the Internet
Set up a wireless, broadband, or dial-up connection to the Internet

3 In the "Connect to the Internet" window, check on "No, create a new connection"

Do you want to use a connection that you already have?

⊙ No, create a new connection

4 Click on the Next button

Next

5 Click on the Wireless option

6 Click on a wireless network

Select a network to connect to

NETGEAR   Unsecured network

7 Click on the Connect button

8 The "Connect to the Internet" window notifies you if
the connection has been successful

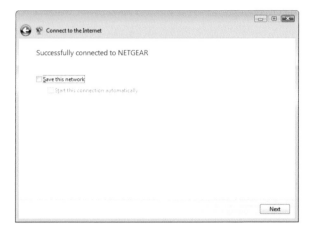

Hot tip

If the connection to
the Internet is not
successful, close down
the Network and
Sharing Center and
then reopen it and try
again. If it still does
not work, turn off the
router and then turn it
back on again.

161

9 Click on the Next button

10 Click on the Next button

11 Click on the "Browse the Internet now" button to
browse the Internet with the new wireless connection

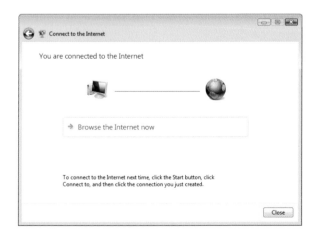

Connecting to a network

A network really comes into its own when more than one computer can be connected to it. It can then be used to share documents between the computers and also allow different people to share a single Internet connection. To connect a computer to an existing network:

1 Access the Control Panel and click on the Network and Internet link

Network and Internet
View network status and tasks
Set up file sharing

2 Click on the Network and Sharing Center link

Network and Sharing Center
View network status and tasks   Connect to a network
View network computers and devices   Add a device to the network
Set up file sharing

3 In the Network and Sharing Center, click on the "Connect to a network" link

Connect to a network

4 Click on an existing network name (this will be the name of the router that was assigned when it was connected)

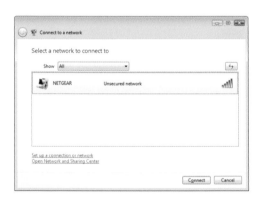

5 Click on the Connect button

Connect

6 If the network connection is made, the following message is displayed

Connect to a network

Successfully connected to NETGEAR

Beware

If a network is shown as being unsecured, this means that it is not password-protected and anyone within range of the router can connect to the network.

7 Click on the Close button

8 The network connection is displayed in the Network and Sharing Center window

Disconnecting

If you want to disconnect from an existing network (so that other people do not have access to your Public documents, for instance), this can be done in a similar way to connecting in the first place. To do this:

1 In the Network and Sharing Center, click on the "Connect to a network" link

2 Click on an existing network name

3 Click on the Disconnect button **Disconnect**

4 A confirmation window appears. Click on the Disconnect option if this is what you want to do

➜ Disconnect
To re-connect to this network in the future, select it from the list and click connect

Wi-Fi networking

Wi-Fi stands for Wireless Fidelity and it is one of the buzzwords in the networking world. Wi-Fi is a method of sending electronic data over wireless networks, and essentially it is a means for providing wireless Internet access at high speeds in public places.

Wi-Fi works through large antennae that transmit powerful radio signals over a certain range, say 100 yards. The antennae are then connected to a central device through which a high-speed Internet connection can be passed. These hotspots can then be used by users with wireless devices, such as a laptop, to connect to the Internet.

Use of Wi-Fi hotspots is free in some cases, or there may be a fee payable, depending on how long you use the service for. Payment is usually made by credit card on a payment page when you first connect to the Wi-Fi hotspot.

Originally, Wi-Fi hotspots were available in areas such as airports, cafes, libraries and hotels. However, there is now a move in many places to create city-wide Wi-Fi hotspots. This is done by creating what is known as a mesh network. This involves numerous antennae that are attached to lamp-posts or road signs around the city. All of the antennae are then connected together so that the hotspot extends across the whole area where there are antennae. As with smaller hotspots, some of these mesh hotspots are proposed to be free to use, while others will require payment. Obviously this is of considerable interest to any mobile user of the Internet, as it will become possible to access it with a wireless laptop from an increasing number of public areas. There are some potential drawbacks to widespread Wi-Fi access, such as variable coverage in different locations and some questions about how the service providers are going to make money. However, for users it is an exciting development that will make the possession of a wireless laptop all the more worthwhile and productive.

If your laptop is equipped to connect wirelessly to a home network then it can also connect to a Wi-Fi one.

Don't forget

A payment page of a hotspot provider is sometimes known as the "landing page".

About hotspots

A hotspot is the name for a Wi-Fi area that provides high-speed Internet access for users of suitably-equipped wireless devices. These are usually over relatively short distances and include coffee shops, restaurants and airports. Anyone with a sufficiently powerful wireless router can set up a hotspot, and this is similar to giving people access to your own home network.

Finding free hotspots

Thankfully, the majority of hotspots around the world are free to use, but it is not always obvious where they are. However, the Web can help solve this problem because there are several online directories that list free hotspots around the world. To find these, type "free hotspots" into your favorite search engine on the Web. (If you want to refine your search, enter a location or city name too.) Some sites to look at are:

- Free-hotspot.com at www.free-hotspot.com

- Wi-Fi FreeSpot at www.wififreespot.com

- The HotSpot Haven at www.hotspothaven.com

- Wi-Here at www.wi-here.com (UK)

These sites offer lists of free hotspots by countries, regions and cities. Click on the links to see the free hotspots.

Using hotspots

When it comes to using a hotspot to connect to the Internet in a public place, the process is very similar to connecting to your own home network and Internet connection:

1. Find a location where there is a Wi-Fi hotspot

2. Click on the Network and Sharing Center link

3. In the Network and Sharing Center, click on the "Connect to a network" link (see page 162)

...cont'd

4 The available wireless networks will be listed. This should include the one belonging to the provider of the hotspot

5 Select a network

6 Click on the Connect button   **Connect**

7 In some cases there may be a code that has to be entered to connect to the hotspot (this can be obtained from the establishment providing the hotspot)

8 Confirmation will appear that you are connecting to the wireless hotspot. After this you can start surfing the Web in the usual way

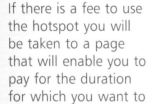

10 Troubleshooting

Viruses are the scourge of the computing world and this chapter shows how to best defend against any malicious programs. It also covers updating your system software and backing up your data.

Protecting against viruses

One of the most important considerations for any computer user is to make sure that they have suitable protection against malicious programs that can infect their machine and compromise its operation and potentially damage or erase folders and files. Windows Vista comes with some built-in protection against viruses, malware and spyware (see following pages) but it is also a good idea to have additional protection in the form of anti-virus software. There are several products on the market and three to look at are:

- McAfee at www.mcafee.com

- Norton at www.symantec.com

- Kaspersky at www.kaspersky.com

Using anti-virus software

Most anti-virus software works in a similar way:

Don't forget

When you buy an anti-virus program you will usually have to pay an annual subscription. This will enable you to keep downloading the latest virus protection files (definitions) to combat new viruses as they appear.

Beware

New viruses are being released all of the time so it is important that you scan for them on a daily basis.

1 Open your chosen program to access its features

2 Any potential problems are identified along with the action required

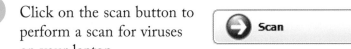

3 Click on the scan button to perform a scan for viruses on your laptop

4 The progress of the scan, along with any potential problems, is displayed here as it is taking place

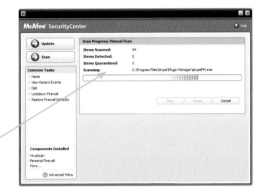

5 Click on the update button to get the latest virus definitions, i.e. the means to stop the latest viruses that have been identified. Updates can usually be set to be performed automatically

> **Update**

6 Once a successful scan has taken place you will be informed that your laptop is protected

> **Am I Protected?** Yes
> Your computer protection services are enabled and up-to-date. No action is required.

Internet and networks

Anti-virus software can also warn you about potential unwanted access to your laptop from the Internet or another user on a network:

1 The anti-virus program will alert you when access is being sought by types of programs on the Internet or from a network

> **Program Requests Internet Access**

2 Select how you want to deal with the request for access

Using a firewall

A firewall is a program that can be used to help stop malicious programs, such as viruses and spyware, from entering your laptop. It acts like a barrier around your laptop and aims to repel any items that is does not trust (these usually come from the Web).

Firewalls can be purchased along with anti-virus software but there is also one that comes pre-installed with Windows Vista. To use this:

Don't forget

If you have an anti-virus program it will probably also have its own firewall. However, it is worth using the Windows Vista one too, for added protection.

170

1 Click on the Start button and access the Control Panel

2 Click on the Security link

Security
Check for updates
Check this computer's security status
Allow a program through Windows Firewall

3 Click on the Windows Firewall link

Windows Firewall
Turn Windows Firewall on or off
Allow a program through Windows Firewall

4 By default, the firewall should be turned on, i.e. protecting your laptop

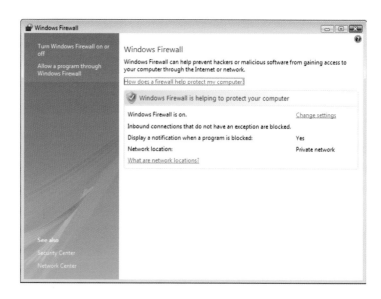

5 If the firewall is not on, click on the "Change settings" link

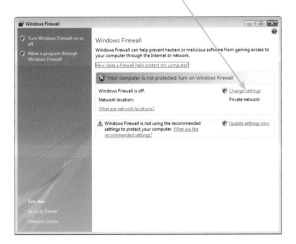

Beware

If you turn off the firewall you will keep getting system messages telling you that you should turn it back on again.

6 Check on the "On (recommended)" box to turn on the firewall

Windows Firewall can help prevent hackers or malicious software from gaining access to your computer through the Internet or a network.

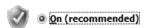

This setting blocks all outside sources from connecting to this computer, except for those unblocked on the Exceptions tab.

7 Click on the OK button

8 The Windows Firewall window indicates that the firewall is turned on

Windows Firewall is on.

Windows Defender

Another option for stopping malicious software entering your laptop is Windows Defender, which can check for spyware and similar types of programs. To use this:

1 Click on the Start button and access the Control Panel

2 Click on the Security link

3 Click on the Windows Defender link

4 The Windows Defender window contains details for scanning your laptop and viewing the results

5 Click on the Scan button to perform a scan on your laptop

6 Once the scan is completed the following message will appear if no malicious programs are detected

No unwanted or harmful software detected.

Your computer is running normally.

7 Click on the Tools button

8 Click on the Options link

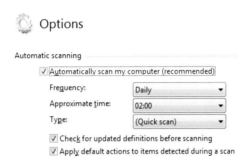

Settings

Options
Choose how you want
Windows Defender to
run

9 Set options
for how you
want Windows
Defender to
operate

Options

Automatic scanning

☑ Automatically scan my computer (recommended)

Frequency: Daily

Approximate time: 02:00

Type: (Quick scan)

☑ Check for updated definitions before scanning
☑ Apply default actions to items detected during a scan

10 Click on the Save button and return
to the Windows Defender window

 Save

11 Click on the
"Quarantined
items" link

Tools

Quarantined items
Remove or restore software that
Windows Defender has prevented
from running

12 Any programs that have been stopped will be
displayed here

Don't forget

If any items are
quarantined you will
be given options for
how to deal with them
and remove them
from your laptop.

173

User Account Controls

One of the features in Vista that is aimed at stopping malicious files or programs being downloaded onto your laptop is called the User Account Controls. This produces a warning window when a variety of actions are performed, such as certain programs being run. However, after time this can become counterproductive: the window can appear so frequently that it is okayed without thinking, just to get rid of it. If this becomes too annoying, it is possible to disable the User Account Controls so that the warning windows do not appear. To do this:

Don't forget

The User Account Controls can also be accessed from within the Other Security Settings section of the Security Center.

174

Beware

If you turn off the User Account Controls your computer may be more vulnerable to infection from unauthorized programs. However, if you have anti-virus software running, this should pick up any of these problems.

1 Click on the Start button and access the Control Panel

2 Click on the User Accounts and Family Safety link and then the User Accounts link

User Accounts
Change your account picture

3 Click on the "Turn User Account Control on or off" link

4 By default, the "Use User Account Control (UAC) to help protect your computer" box is checked. Uncheck it to disable the User Account Controls. Click on the OK button and restart your laptop for the new setting to take effect

Security Center

For all of the security settings on your laptop it is useful to be able to see them in one location. This can be done with the Security Center, which also enables you to alter these settings if required. To use the Security Center:

1 Click on the Start button and access the Control Panel

2 Click on the Security link

3 Click on the Security Center link

4 All of the current essential security settings are displayed

5 Click on this button to view the settings for a particular item

Check settings ●

6 If required, select one of the options to alter the settings in the Security Center

Don't forget

An item with a green banner is fully protected and up to date. An amber banner means that there are some issues relating to this item. A red banner means that the required settings are not in place and your laptop could be at risk.

Updating software

One of the best ways to try and keep your laptop as secure as possible is to make sure that your system software is fully up to date. This is because there are frequent updates that repair security problems that come to light with the operating system and associated programs. With Vista, updates can be downloaded and installed automatically through the use of the Windows Update function:

1 Click on the Start button and access the Control Panel

2 Click on either the Security link or the System and Maintenance link

3 Click on the Windows Update link

Windows Update
Turn automatic updating on or off | Check for updates |
View installed updates

Don't forget

Updates are released on a regular basis so you should be looking for new ones on at least a weekly basis.

4 The Windows Update window displays any updates that are available

5 Click on the "Check for updates" link to manually check for new updates

6 Click on the "Change settings" link to alter how Windows Update operates

7 Check on the "Install updates automatically" button

8 Enter the timing for when you want the updates to be downloaded and installed

9 Click on the OK button

OK

Additional updates

As well as Windows updates, it is also possible to get updates for other devices such as printer drivers and other hardware devices that are connected to your laptop and may require additional software to run properly. To check for these types of updates:

1 In the Windows Update window, click on the "View available updates" link

Install updates

View available updates

2 The available updates are listed. Check on the box next to the one that you want to install

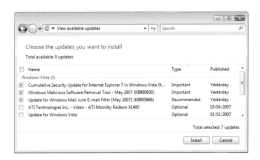

3 Click on the Install button

Install

177

Backing up

The security settings in Vista are designed to try and protect your laptop as much as possible and ensure that you don't lose any valuable data. However, no system is infallible and sometimes malicious programs, or human error, can cause the loss of files and documents on your laptop. Because of this it is important that you have a robust procedure in place for backing up your information and also have the means to restore it if it does get deleted or corrupted. The first step is to make sure your computer files are backed up. To do this:

1. Click on the Start button and access the Control Panel

2. Click on the System and Maintenance link

System and Maintenance
Get started with Windows
Back up your computer

3. Click on the Backup and Restore Center link

Backup and Restore Center
Back up your computer | Restore files from backup

4. In the Backup and Restore Center, click on the "Back up files" button

Back up files

5. Select an option for where you want to back up your files

6. Click on the Next button

Next

7 Select the disc on which you want the files to be backed up

8 Click on the Next button

9 The Back Up Files window shows the types of files that can be backed up

10 Check on the boxes for all of the file types that you want to include in the backup process

11 Click on the Next button

12 Options can be set for how the backup is performed after the first one has been done. Click here to select settings for each option

...cont'd

13 Click on the "Save settings and exit" button

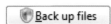

14 Click on "Back up files"

 Back up files

15 For a backup onto a CD or DVD you will be prompted to insert a blank disc into your CD or DVD writer. Do so and click on the OK button

 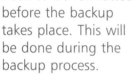
16 The following window will be displayed as the backup is taking place

17 Once the backup has been completed this window will be displayed

18 Click on the Close button

Close

Restoring files

Once files have been backed up they should be kept in a safe place, preferably in a different location from the original files, i.e. the laptop itself. If the original files ever get deleted or corrupted, they can be restored from the backup disc, or network location. To do this:

1 Open the Backup and Restore Center from the Control Panel

2 In the "Restore files" section, click on the "Restore files" button

> **Restore files**

3 Select a backup from which you want to restore the files

> What do you want to restore?
>
> ◉ Files from the latest backup
>
> ○ Files from an older backup

4 Click on the Next button

> **Next**

5 The Restore Files window contains options for selecting which items you want to restore

6 Click on an "Add" button

> **Add folders...**

...cont'd

7 Select a folder (or file)

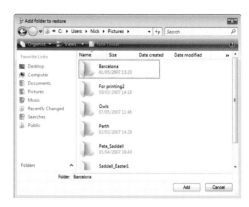

8 Click on the Add button   Add

9 The selected folder(s) or file(s) are displayed in the Restore Files window

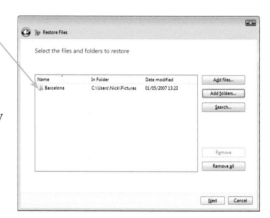

10 Click on the Next button   Next

11 Check on this button to restore the folder(s) or file(s) to their original location; or   ◉ In the original location

12 Check on this button to restore them to a different location   ◉ In the following location:

13 Click on the Browse button   Browse...

14 Select a destination for the restored items and click on the OK button

15 The selected location for the restored items is shown here

◉ In the **f**ollowing location:

C:\Users\Nick\

16 Click on the "Start restore" button

Start restore

17 This window is displayed as the restore is taking place

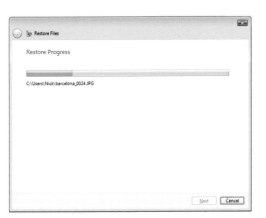

18 This window is displayed once the items have been successfully restored

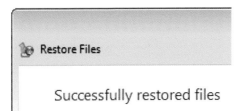

19 Click on the Finish button

Finish

Hot tip

If you are at all worried about copying over existing files, restore the files from the backup disc to a different location from the original one.

System Restore

Inevitably when working with your laptop you will come across occasions when it behaves erratically. This could be because of a program that has been loaded or software (driver) that has been loaded for an external device, such as a printer. However, with Vista it is possible to try and rectify the problem by restoring the settings of your laptop to an earlier date. This does not affect any of your personal files or folders, but it can help the laptop perform better by taking it back to a date before the problem started. To do this:

Hot tip

System Restore is a good option to use if your laptop starts to perform erratically after you have installed a new program.

1 Click on the Start button and access the Control Panel. Click on the System Maintenance link

2 Click on the Backup and Restore Center link

Backup and Restore Center
Back up your computer   Restore files from backup

3 In the Tasks panel, click on the "Repair Windows using System Restore" link

Tasks
Repair Windows using System Restore

4 The System Restore window has options for when you want your laptop restored to

5 Click on the "Recommended restore" button to undo the most recent changes that you have made to your laptop

Recommended restore:

Select this option to undo the most recent update, driver, or software installation if you think it is causing problems.

05/05/2007 10:28:37 Install: Windows Update

Choose a different restore point

6   Click on the Next button   Next >

7   The System Restore window has the time to which your laptop will be restored

Confirm your restore point

Time: 05/05/2007 10:28:37

Description: Install: Windows Update

> **Hot tip**
>
> Always start with the most recent System Restore point to see if this fixes the problem. If not, use a more distant restore point.

8   Click on the Finish button   Finish

Creating a restore point

As well as selecting a restore point that has been created by Windows for your laptop, it is also possible to create your own restore point. You might want to do this before you install a new program or a driver for a device such as a printer. To create your own restore point:

1   In the Backup and Restore Center click on the "Create a restore point or change settings" link

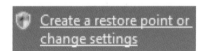

2   The System Properties window has options for creating your own restore point

3   Click on the Create button   Create...

185

...cont'd

4 Enter a name for the restore point (the time and date will be added automatically). Click on the Create button

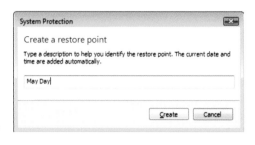

5 The following window appears if the restore point has been created. Click on the OK button

6 To view the restore point, click on the "Choose a different restore point" button in the System Restore window (see Step 4 on page 184) and click on the Next button

7 The restore point is added to the list of restore points that have been created automatically by Windows. Click on the Next button to restore your laptop to this point

Index

M

N